WRITING
ABOUT
ART

HENRY M. SAYRE

Oregon State University

PRENTICE HALL, Englewood Cliffs, New Jersey 07632

Library of Congress Cataloging-in-Publication Data

Sayre, Henry M.,
   Writing about art / Henry M. Sayre.
     p.   cm.
   Bibliography p.
   ISBN 0-13-969767-5
   1. Art criticism--Authorship.   I. Title.
N7476.S29 1989
808'.0667--dc19

88-27615
                                              CIP

Editorial/production supervision
  and interior design: Alison D. Gnerre
Manufacturing buyer: Raymond Keating

Cover Art: "Ambiguous Zones of a Lemon" from *The Mechanism of Meaning* by Arakawa and Madeline H. Gins, Abbeville Press, 1988, p. 21; Matisse, "Decorative Figure on an Ornamental Background, 1925, Musée national d'art moderne, Paris, France.

 © 1989 by Prentice-Hall, Inc.
A Division of Simon & Schuster
Englewood Cliffs, New Jersey 07632

Printed in the United States of America

10 9 8 7 6 5 4

ISBN 0-13-969767-5

Prentice-Hall International (UK) Limited, *London*
Prentice-Hall of Australia Pty. Limited, *Sydney*
Prentice-Hall Canada Inc., *Toronto*
Prentice-Hall Hispanoamericana, S.A., *Mexico*
Prentice-Hall of India Private Limited, *New Delhi*
Prentice-Hall of Japan, Inc., *Tokyo*
Simon & Schuster Asia Pte. Ltd., *Singapore*
Editora Prentice-Hall do Brasil, Ltda., *Rio de Janeiro*

CONTENTS

PREFACE

As a teacher of undergraduate courses in art appreciation and history, I have always felt that one of the most important activities students engage in is *writing*. It is my conviction that the better, and the sooner, students can write about what they see, the better they will see. To write about art is to engage in the best process I know for organizing—even recognizing—your thoughts and feelings about the visual world.

This book, then, is addressed to you, the art student, in the hope that it will help you to write about art more effectively and thus teach you, through the process of writing, how to see works of art in more meaningful and lasting terms. Many of you are already effective writers, many of you may still lack the confidence you need to feel that you write well, but if you are reading this book, you almost surely find the problem of writing about art a vexing one. If, after all, the visual arts expressed the same things in the same way as the verbal arts, then why would anyone bother to paint or sculpt or take photographs in the first place? Most people feel that images tend to "say" things that words can't. For them, being asked to write about a visual image is like being asked to express the inexpressible.

Without denying the uniqueness of the visual experience, let me suggest that works of art are a form of address, directed at you, their audience. Like most forms of address, they demand a response. To write about a work of art is to respond in what for most of us is the most readily available means. In order to demonstrate the kinds of response a work of art might generate, I have written, in this book, about works of art that have excited me—and continue to excite me—and I have also included several responses to works of art written by my students. This book is not, however, an art appreciation text. It is meant to supplement your regular textbook. Nor does it address general conventions of writing—questions of grammar, sentence and paragraph construction, and so on. Students who need help with these skills can seek that help elsewhere. This book discusses conventions that are particular to writing about art, and it offers several approaches designed to help you organize your thoughts and shape your feelings about art, approaches applicable to your writing in general, whatever the subject matter.

I hope that this book convinces you that writing about art is a rewarding and pleasurable experience, an act of exploration and discovery in some ways comparable to the creative act itself. At the very least, this book should help you to write better papers in art appreciation courses and throughout your career as a student of art history. In the end, I hope the book increases your confidence—and joy—in the process of writing itself.

LIST OF ILLUSTRATIONS

INTRODUCTION
The Process of Seeing and Writing

Ever since I began teaching art appreciation and art history, at least once each term a student has tried to excuse a poorly written essay by saying, "Sorry, but I'm right-brained." Scientists have long known that injury to the left side of the brain can severely impair verbal ability. Studies in the last two or three decades have further indicated that while the right side of the brain shows little concern with matters of logic and language, it is the repository of intuition, dreams, and images. The right side of the brain is the artist's domain, and it has become fashionable, especially among certain art students, to cultivate a "right-brained" persona. It is an integral part of their definition of themselves as artists. Artists, their argument goes, think differently than the rest of us. They are exempt from the world of logic and words. We of the left-brained populace should be content to let them drift in their sea of unbounded associations and free-floating images. Artists don't talk (let alone write)—they make art.

However valid the characterization of artists as right-brained, nonverbal people may or may not be, too often the right brain is championed at the expense of the left. Most studies have shown that, barring physical impairment or injury, each of us can—and should—develop the capacities of both sides. Of all contemporary painters, probably Jackson Pollock did more to

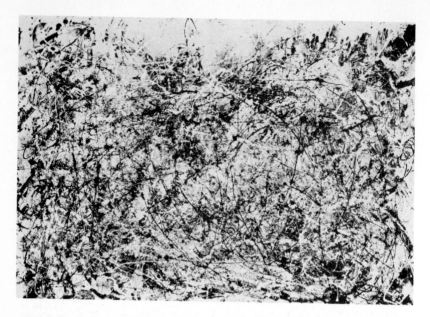

Figure 1   Jackson Pollock, *Number 1, 1948*, 1948. Oil on canvas, 68 inches by 8 feet, 8 inches. Collection, The Museum of Modern Art, New York. Purchase.

promote the artist's right-brained persona than anyone. And, on first view, his work seems almost certain to promote verbal incapacity in its audience as well. Pollock so disliked language, at least as it related to his painting, that as often as not he refused to title his work, assigning each painting a number instead (Fig. 1). Early in his career Pollock had so frustrated his psychiatrist with his nonverbal behavior that his therapy was in jeopardy. Communication between the two became possible only when Pollock revealed that he was, more or less routinely, illustrating his psychic condition in his notebooks. (His psychiatrist was able to talk to him upon seeing his drawings, to convert his images into words. Pollock's therapy, in fact, depended upon that transformation of images into words.) If Pollock was unwilling to talk to his psychiatrist, whom he claimed to trust, he was even less willing to speak in public. Only when he drank—and his reputation as a man of the bottle was unmatched in New York in the early 1950s—did he talk in public, and then often only to let loose with such a string of obscenities that most of his colleagues at the famous Cedar Bar, the artists' hangout he most frequented, greatly preferred his silence. He soon developed a reputation as, alternately, a great, hulking, hugely talented mute and a loud, pushy, famously abusive drunkard. The drunkard, as it turned out, couldn't paint. It was the silent Pollock, everyone knew, who was the artist.

There was at least as much shadow as substance to Pollock's quietude, however. "It's a myth that he wasn't verbal," his wife, the painter Lee Krasner said in an interview in 1967, a decade after he died in a car accident near his home on Long Island. "He could be hideously verbal when he wanted to be. . . . He was lucid, intelligent; it was simply that he didn't want to talk art. If he was quiet, it was because he didn't believe in talking, he believed in *doing*."[1] There is probably no better explanation of the "meaning" of the many untitled and numbered paintings in the body of Pollock's work. His refusal to title or discuss his paintings *tells* us something about them—that we are to see in them, as a record of Pollock's *"doing,"* the activity of making art itself. As a matter of fact, we can detect in Pollock's conscious refusal to put words to his images a choice that takes on a particularly American tone, for born and raised in the West he always conceived of himself as something of a cowboy. Certainly in New York he considered himself a rough, tough Westerner, the silent hero who rides into town, takes care of business, and rides out again. He was the art world's Gary Cooper.

The process of writing about art involves the recognition that even when one is confronted by a work of art that is so obscure that it seems impenetrable, that looks as hopelessly confusing or willfully pointless as a Jackson Pollock must appear to the untrained observer, a certain fabric of choices and decisions is nevertheless always apparent. For Pollock to paint as he did, he had to *choose* not to paint in a traditionally representational way. He had to *choose* to suppress or reject traditional subject matter. He had to *choose* to paint on very large canvases instead of small ones, to create a design of scribbles and curves and arabesques as opposed to a grid of straight lines and geometric shapes, to title his paintings or not. When you write about art, begin by identifying these choices, and then proceed to the problem of determining *why* an artist made the choices he or she did.

The process of writing about art, then, begins with recognizing that certain decisions have been made and wondering why. Chapter 1, "Choosing an Image," is about how to put yourself in the best position to recognize these decisions. Viewing a work of art and writing about it involves, of course, some initial decision making on your own part. You have to ask yourself, "Among the myriad possibilities displayed in the museum or gallery, which is the work of art I can write about most effectively?" Then, having made an intelligent choice of your own, you can begin to determine what meaningful choices the artist has made. Chapter 2, "Using Visual Information," is a summary of the visual elements from which an artist might choose. The intention of the chapter is to help you recognize what sorts of visual information might be important for you to write about. It is meant only as a supplement to the many discussions of visual elements in the various art appreciation texts available, which can provide you with a fuller understanding of these elements. In Chapter 3, "Responding to the Verbal Frame," the problem of words and their relation to the image is addressed. All images in art are surrounded by words—in their titles, in accompanying exhibition materials, in critical and art historical discussion. Some works of art even contain words. It is, of course, not always necessary to consider all of the verbal baggage an art work carries with it. Depending upon the nature of the essay you have to write, you may or may not want to consult secondary sources such as critical commentaries or monographs for help in understanding the image. Some of this verbal material is essential, however, and, in one way or another, it all can help you begin to think about your own verbal approach to the work of art.

Chapter 4, "Working with Words and Images," is about the crucial activity of writing itself. One of the first things you will discover, if you don't already know it, is that images somehow seem to resist words. It could even be argued that paintings get painted in order to say things words can't, and that similarly poems get written to describe emotions images can't convey. This is the point, in fact, of Martha Rosler's *The Bowery in Two Inadequate Descriptive Systems* (Fig. 2). The work consists of a series of words used to describe the drunks and winos of New York City's famous skid row juxtaposed to photographic images of the place itself. However, the words convey nothing of the place, its dilapidation and decay, while the images are not only unpopulated but void of social content. They are, instead, formally interesting, possessing an artistic and aesthetic dimension which the words, in their very colloquial, matter-of-fact way, deny. There is a gulf here between word and image that appears very large indeed.

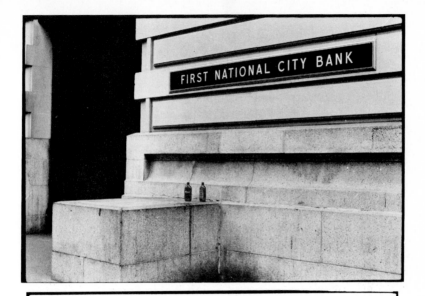

Figure 2   Martha Rosler, from *The Bowery in Two Inadequate Descriptive Systems*, 1974–1975. Courtesy the artist.

Another way that this gulf between word and image will manifest itself to you is that the words you choose to describe or interpret a work of art, especially in the first stages of writing, will often seem *reductive*. While whatever you have to say might well be true, you will likely feel that it is true only to a degree. Most images are more ambiguous than you are at first willing to admit. You will want to pin them down, understand them, and you will tend to think that understanding is itself unambiguous. But if you agree that one of the primary reasons to write about art is to *interpret* the meaning of the images it presents, and if you reflect on the word *interpretation* for a moment, you can see that almost by definition a work's meaning is never single, is always open to discussion, even heated debate. Thus Frederic Edwin Church's monumental painting of a South American volcano in eruption, *Cotopaxi, Ecuador* (Fig. 24), painted in 1862, has sometimes been read as an awe-inspiring transcription of the sublime power of the natural world, as an expression of the Divine in nature, following the lead of Ralph Waldo Emerson's transcendental philosophy. It has also been interpreted as an allegory of the American Civil War in which the forces of the North still can be seen shining forth through the smoke of the furious onslaught of the South. Finally, in more psychological terms, it can be seen as symbolic of sexual conflict and union. Perhaps, in fact, all of these readings contribute to the power of the painting, which was indeed one of the most popular of its day.

On the other hand, the "openness" of images to a variety of readings and interpretations has been wonderfully parodied by the painter Arakawa in a book-length collaboration with the poet Madeline H. Gins entitled *The Mechanism of Meaning*. In *The Ambiguous Zones of a Lemon* (Fig. 3) what is labeled the "image of a lemon" looks more like a lime, the "animal's lemon" like a potato, the "impression of a lemon" like a fountain pen, and so on. There are, as the title suggests, ambiguous zones between each statement and its representation. To say of a long brown rectangle, "This is a lemon," is to leap across the conceptual gap between word and image so capriciously that any relation between the two is lost. What Arakawa points out is the danger of interpretation—the point where the relation of word to image becomes arbitrary. Writing about works of art always involves walking the line between the image's openness, or its susceptibility to interpretation, and its integrity, or its resistance to arbitrary and capricious readings. We must continually test our reading of a work of art against the image itself. We must determine if it is complete enough (if it recognizes the full range of possible meanings the work might possess) and, *at the same time*, we must ask ourselves if it violates the image, misrepresents it.

Writing About Art is meant to help you learn to test your interpretations of works of art through the process of writing about them. Before you begin to explore that process, however, let me make one final point. Writing about works of art may

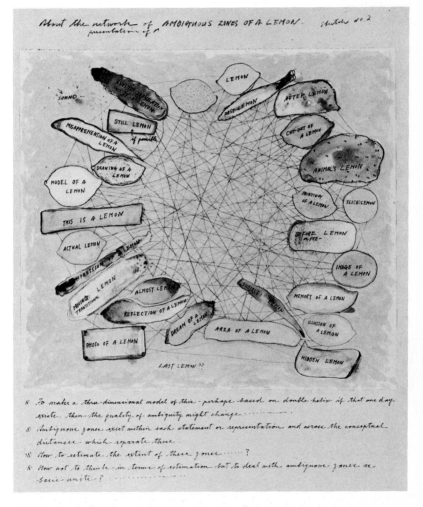

Figure 3   Arakawa and Madeline H. Gins, from *The Mechanism of Meaning*. Abbeville Press, 1988, p. 21. Reproduced by permission of the publisher.

seem to you a very specialized, even esoteric and rarefied, kind of activity. It may seem to have little to do with the important business of getting on with your life. It can, however, teach you some very important critical habits—that is, it can make you question what you see. Most professors are not nearly so interested in seeing you make the "right" interpretation of a work of art—they recognize a certain "openness" and amplitude in the work—as they are in seeing you ask hard questions about the work itself and about your responses to it. My primary goal as an educator—and I share this goal with many others—is to teach you to be actively engaged with your world, not passively receptive to it, to be at once critical and self-critical. Writing about art is one way to begin this larger process. The skills you develop will be, I promise, applicable to whatever endeavor you choose to pursue in your life.

1

CHOOSING AN IMAGE
How to Select a Work of Art
to Write About

VISITING MUSEUMS
AND GALLERIES

When you enter a museum, how do you feel, and do your feelings affect the way you see? This is not so much to ask whether you feel happy or sad, bored or confused—though your mood and temperament can obviously affect your perception of things—but whether the museum itself reminds you of a church or a library, a lecture hall or a department store. In studies conducted in the late 1960s two French scholars discovered that 66 percent of all manual workers, 45 percent of all skilled and blue-collar workers, and 30.5 percent of the professional and upper managerial class most closely associated museums with churches. A large group of the skilled and white-collar workers—34 percent—felt that the museum was most analogous to the library. Of the professionals and managers, 28 percent likened the museum to the library. Only small percentages of each group likened the museum to lecture halls or department stores, but a large number of professionals, nearly 20 percent of them, felt that a museum was like none of these other institutions; a museum, they must have felt, is most like itself.[1]

These figures can be interpreted in any number of useful and interesting ways, but my point is a simple one: for most people, the museum possesses an aura, a mystique, which literally transforms the work of art. The museum removes art from the context of everyday life. Everywhere there are signs— "Please Do Not Touch the Works of Art"—which imply to many people not only the "purity" and "sanctity" of art itself, but by extension their own relative corruption. Like the library, the museum demands the *silent* contemplation and study of its objects. It is the kind of space in which people feel compelled to whisper, reverently, and in which parents feel obliged to collar their children, put them on their best behavior, and demand their submissive attention.

People, then, tend to take museums rather seriously—perhaps too seriously. Marcel Duchamp, in one of the most important gestures in the history of twentieth-century art, pointed this fact out when he signed a common urinal, which he had purchased at an ordinary plumbing store, with the pseudonym R. Mutt, entitled it *Fountain,* and submitted it to the 1917 Independents Exhibition in New York City (Fig. 4). The urinal was at first rejected by the jury, which no doubt considered it simultaneously ludicrous, obscene, and banal, but when it became known that "R. Mutt" was Duchamp, the piece was installed in the show, behind a partition. Soon critics waxed on about its purity of line and the graceful symmetry of its structure. In the

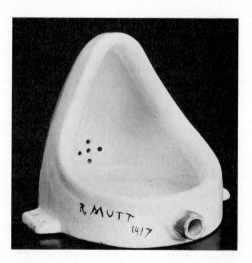

Figure 4   Marcel Duchamp, *Fountain,* 1917. Selected object, 24 inches high. Courtesy Sidney Janis Gallery, New York.

spirit of the piece, one poet would write, "Would not life be lovelier if you were constantly overjoyed by the sublimely pure concavity of your wash bowls? The tubular dynamics of your cigarette?"[2] Wouldn't it be nice, in other words, if we approached all things in life with the attentiveness we habitually give to works of art? Wouldn't it be nice if we saw the world *aesthetically*?

Duchamp's point was that in order to see aesthetically, most of us—those who aren't poets and artists—need to be prodded, and what jogs our aesthetic sense most readily is the museum itself. When we enter its doors, we somehow agree to look at things differently. A urinal, for instance, might lose its functional purpose; we might even approach it as sculpture. *Context*, in short, plays a large role in determining the way we see. And the power of Duchamp's piece lies in the fact that it forces us to recognize that the aesthetic dimension of a thing might be more a function of where we see it than of any quality inherent in the thing itself.

Furthermore, each museum, sometimes each gallery in a museum, has its own unique aura. Seeing art in the Guggenheim Museum (Fig. 5) is not the same experience as seeing it down the street at the Metropolitan (Fig. 6). The manifest differences in

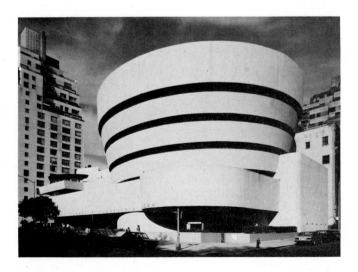

Figure 5   Exterior view, Solomon R. Guggenheim Museum, New York. Photo David Heald.

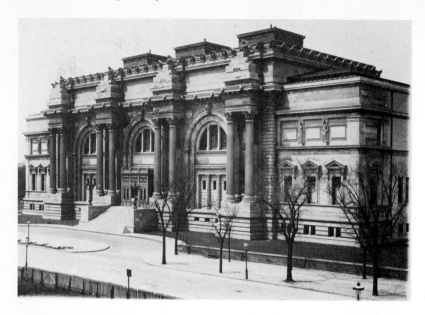

Figure 6   Facade, Metropolitan Museum of Art, New York. Courtesy The Metropolitan Museum of Art.

their respective architectures—the Met's traditional neoclassical facade, designed by Richard Morris Hunt and completed in 1902, as opposed to the highly inventive modernism of Frank Lloyd Wright's Guggenheim, with the spiral design of its central gallery—create two different sets of expectation.

For instance, the innocent museum-goer would expect to see at the Guggenheim modern and contemporary works of art, and at the Met more traditional types of things. One would be more likely to overhear exasperated utterances of disgust before an abstract (or even semi-abstract) painting hanging in the galleries of the Met than if that same painting were hanging in the Guggenheim. As a building, the Guggenheim selects its audience (and so does the Met). It announces its contents.

In the same manner, the walls and the frames that surround works of art influence the ways in which we see them. An ornate, gilded frame seems more appropriate to a Renaissance painting, whereas a thin white, silver, or black strip of metal seems best around contemporary works. If a starkly geometric abstract painting is presented in an elaborate baroque frame, our sense of it changes dramatically. The tension between it and its environment is heightened. It seems to announce its difference. It places itself outside its context. Such effects may or may not be the intention of the artist. It may be that the collector, or even the curator, has decided to accentuate the painting's independence from its surroundings. The reasons may be many, and legitimate, but it is important to realize that such effects influence the way we see.

One of the most interesting examples of this effect is the Lehmann Wing of the Metropolitan Museum. Here a not altogether significant collection of Renaissance and Impressionist paintings, as well as furnishings of all kinds, are housed in a replica of the Lehmann home. But the question is, what kind of experience is it to look at paintings in this context? Are we seeing the paintings? Or are we, more accurately, recreating for ourselves what it must have been like for Lehmann to see them? Hasn't the Metropolitan really provided us with a lesson in connoisseurship, allowing us not so much a chance to appreciate the paintings in their own right as to experience what it must be like to be wealthy enough to own them?

A less obvious but equally telling example is the so-called "white room" effect which dominates the display of contemporary art. It is important to remember that many contemporary paintings are painted with just such an environment in mind; it is assumed that they will end up surrounded by a more or less pure, immaculate, and virgin space. Though a medieval or Renaissance crucifixion might have been painted with an entirely different end in mind for the work—perhaps a cathedral or chapel—the effect is not very different. Both environments, the church and the white room, create an atmosphere of *attention*, one could even say *devotion*. In the white room there is nothing to distract the gaze from the work. More or less by default, it becomes the center of our attention. In the church, particularly in the cathedral, there might be other sources of visual interest—sculpture, stained glass, the very architecture of the place—but it is the centrality of the crucifixion to the Christian tradition, the power of the image itself, that draws our attention to it. Without that image, and what it signifies, the entire edifice which surrounds it would crumble. It could be said, in fact, that what is inherently powerful in a crucifixion becomes a studied *effect* in the white room. The white room manipulates us. It allows us to mistake our attentiveness for something like adoration and worship.

The difficulty here is not so much that we find ourselves adoring and revering works of art—such feelings are perfectly permissible and even noble—and it is not even that we might have been manipulated by the curator or the architect into feeling the way we do, but that as viewers we are plunged into a paradoxical situation which needlessly tends to mystify our experience of the work of art. One of the best analyses of this situation can be found in a series of articles by Brian O'Doherty, originally written for *Artforum* in the mid-1970s, entitled "Inside the White Cube." "The ideal gallery," O'Doherty says,

> subtracts from the artwork all cues that interfere with the fact that it is "art." The work is isolated from everything that would detract from [it]. . . . The outside world must not come in, so windows are usually sealed off. Walls are painted white. The wooden floor is polished so that you click along clinically or carpeted so that you pad soundlessly, resting the feet while the eyes have at the wall. The art is free, as the saying used to go, "to take on its own life."[3]

The art is anything but free, however, and this ambiguity, which is perhaps inevitable, repeats itself in varying forms throughout our experience of it. For although the work of art is technically isolated from things that would interfere with our appreciation of it for its own sake and in its own terms, it perpetually encounters a force "from the outside," one might say, that is always violating its sanctity. It is always meeting the enemy face to face—and it is us.

We all carry all manner of baggage with us when we see works of art, even if it is downright distaste for the particular work of art we happen to be looking at, and what we carry affects what we see, let alone how well we see it. Seeing art, then, is a self-critical as much as it is a critical operation. It involves, absolutely, examining our own prejudices and preconceptions. If the work of art seems distant from us, isolated there on the wall, that is so because, in a certain sense, it needs that protection. Museum histories are rife with examples of the mutilation of works of art. But the work of art needs also to rise above whatever ignorance or misunderstanding we might initially bring to it, even if we aren't about to abuse it physically. It needs to demand our respect. The history of modern art in some ways is the history of the public's initial misapprehension and disapprobation of art it would eventually come to admire and love. Almost everyone today likes Impressionist painting. Yet when it first appeared in France in the 1870s, it was thought laughable, even scandalous. In his 1886 novel, *The Masterpiece,* Emile Zola provides a fictionalized account of the crowd's reaction to an Impressionist painting that more or less summarizes the way in which much of the work of his friends and contemporaries— Manet, Cézanne, Monet, Sisley—was initially received:

> It was one long-drawn-out explosion of laughter, rising in inten-
> sity to hysteria. As soon as they reached the doorway, he saw
> visitors' faces expand with anticipated mirth, their eyes narrow,
> their mouths broaden into a grin, and from every side came
> tempestuous puffings and blowings from fat men, rusty, grating
> whimperings from thin ones, and, dominating all the rest, high-
> pitched, fluty giggles from the women. A group of young men on
> the opposite side of the room were writhing as if their ribs were
> being tickled. One woman had collapsed on to a bench, her knees
> pressed tightly together, gasping, struggling to regain her breath
> behind her handkerchief. . . . The ones who did not laugh lost
> their tempers, taking the overall blueness [of the picture],
> Claude's original way of rendering the effect of daylight, as an
> insult to their intelligence. It was an outrage and should be
> stopped, according to elderly gentlemen who brandished their
> walking sticks in indignation. One very serious individual, as he
> stalked away in anger, was heard announcing to his wife that he
> had no use for bad jokes. . . . It was beginning to look like a riot.
> More and more people kept forcing their way up to the picture,
> and as the heat grew more intense faces grew more and more
> purple.[4]

Context, of course, is playing a large part in determining the reaction of this crowd. The picture they are outraged by describes nature—the effects of daylight—in what is, to them, a new way. It is unlike anything else in their experience. And it is unlike anything else around it. It is hanging, futhermore, in what was known as the Salon des Refusés, an exhibition of all works submitted to the main Salon but refused acceptance by the French Academy. It is, from the point of view of the crowd, the most scandalously bad painting in an exhibition of officially bad painting.

It is perhaps fair to say that one reason we have so little trouble ourselves in seeing paintings such as the one described by Zola as works of great beauty, rather than as objects of deri-sion, is that we are used to seeing a great many of them, together, in the large gallery devoted to Impressionist painting in the Metropolitan Museum, for instance, or in the more intimate space of the Jeu de Paume in Paris (a collection recently transferred to the top floor of the new Musée d'Orsay). Here, seen as a group, the paintings tend to inform one another. We can see for ourselves, in a series of Monet haystacks, how at different times of day, in different seasons of the year, and in different weather, the same scene can dramatically alter in effect. Or we can witness the logical growth of Cézanne's ideas about composition if we compare an early rendering of a particular motif, such as his *Mont Sainte-Victoire* of 1885–87 (Fig. 21), discussed in the next chapter, with a later version of the same scene (Fig. 22).

It is, of course, one of the primary functions of museums to provide just this sort of educational experience, to allow us to see *in context* works of art which in isolation might appear extravagant or ill-considered or even badly executed. Thus any museum or gallery that makes even the slightest pretense at creating a unified or coherent exhibition almost automatically defies the "white cube" effect. (And while one can imagine a show entitled, say, "16 Works in 16 Different Media by 16 Artists None of Whom Know One Another," it would be hard to create an exhibition of more than a single work of art which could avoid at least the aura of some unifying idea or theme.) In commercial galleries, which after all are trying to sell the works they display, this sense of unity and coherence is most readily apparent. The so-called "one-person" show, the staple of the gallery system, almost guarantees a coherent visual effect, and galleries themselves are often known by the particular "look" or style that they champion. A sense of unity can be achieved in any number of ways, however, particularly in the larger context of the museum, where collections are sometimes wildly various and the potential for chaos is markedly greater. Commonly, in museums, works of art are grouped by school or group (the Cubists, for instance, in one room, the Futurists in another), by theme (landscapes or portraits), by nationality and/or historical period (nineteenth-century British or Flemish painting), chronologically (in order to emphasize the historical development of the works), by some critical theory (such as Peter Galassi's "Before Photography" at the Museum of Modern Art in 1981, which argued that the invention of photography in the nineteenth century was made possible by a shift in point of view that had occurred in painting and drawing as early as the middle of the previous century), or by any combination of these ("Nineteenth-Century British Landscape," for instance, or "American Abstraction: Its Roots and Its Legacy").

Curators also often guarantee the continued movement of people through the museum by limiting the number of important or "star" works in any given space. The attention of the visitor is drawn to such works most often by positioning and lighting. If it is a particularly large painting, for instance, the other works in the room will almost always be smaller, and might even be drawings or sketches. A relatively small but important painting might be sumptuously framed, or hung by itself on a given wall, perhaps accompanied by especially elaborate explanatory material.

The museum, in other words, is addressed to *you*. It wants to make art available to you, and it wants you to gather, from your experience, a greater understanding of and appreciation for what you've seen. Although the work of art, and the museum itself, might possess a certain aura of religiosity or sanctity, if we grant the art the respect that is its due, we are free to enter into a dialogue with it, for, like the museum as a whole, each individual work is addressed to its audience, individually and collectively. If you do not allow yourself to be intimidated by the museum, and if you recognize the ways in which your own responses are being manipulated—sometimes to great advantage—by the museum itself, this dialogue can be particularly interesting and worthwhile.

CHOOSING A WORK
TO WRITE ABOUT:
SOME QUESTIONS OF TASTE

One of the best ways to think of the task before you when you are asked to write about art is to approach it as a kind of dialogue between yourself and the work. It is your business, when you write about art, to record this dialogue. But there are dialogues and there are dialogues. You want to avoid having your dialogue turn into a diatribe. Therefore the first rule of thumb is to avoid, if at all possible, writing about something you simply don't like or understand (often these are the same thing).

All too often, when we are confronted by things we do not understand, we react to them in the way that Zola's crowd reacted to the painting in *The Masterpiece*. We are all interested in reading why an authoritative critic dislikes a given work, but we risk appearing uninformed, even boorish, when we criticize what we don't understand. I have received, for instance, many a paper that pointed out how Manet or Picasso was a "bad" painter because he "obviously" didn't understand the laws of perspective. Of course, they *did* understand the laws of perspective but chose to violate those laws in order, among other things, to assert their independence from both traditional painting itself and conventional attitudes about the representational functions of painting. Such papers show not only that the writers are themselves traditional and conventional (not in itself particularly damning), but, more important, that they don't understand the paintings they are writing about.

You are, of course, entitled to your opinion. However, you should recognize the limitations of your opinion, and you should also recognize that in all likelihood your audience— namely your professor—is probably better informed on the subject than you are. This is not to say that you have to force yourself somehow to like all, or most, or even any of the works in a museum or gallery you happen to visit. It is, however, important that you recognize that someone likes them enough to have selected them for exhibition, and that you respect their choice. Thus, it is your business not only to enter into a dialogue with the work of art, but to have a *respectful* dialogue, one that tries to account for the presence of this work of art in the museum itself. In other words, it is a good tactic to neutralize, as much as possible, your own opinions and to account instead for the opinions of others. Say to yourself, "Someone likes this. Why? What's interesting about it?" Quite often you'll find that in accounting for the interest of others, you will become interested yourself.

Sometimes you might find yourself able to write about a work that you're sure you understand completely. For instance, I often give beginning students the opportunity to visit any gallery they choose and to write about any work they want. Huge proportions of students write about a landscape that reminds them of home or—the example is admittedly trite, but it is an actual one—a still life of daisies named "First Love." The problem is that such works are often so accessible and so rudimentary in their appeal, that once you've said, "It reminds me of home," or "It reminds me of my boyfriend who is always giving me daisies," there isn't much left to say. It's certainly not wrong to like images of this kind, but it is important to recognize that, whatever their emotional appeal, they often lack the kind of intellectual richness that other kinds of art possess. Their attraction, furthermore, might be purely personal and may be of little or no interest to anyone but you. At the very least, recognize that there may not be sufficient complexity in them to sustain an interesting essay.

All this implies, of course, that the best works of art to write about usually possess a reasonable *complexity*, that they *challenge* you intellectually, and that they sustain a high level of *interest* on a plane other than the purely personal. In my own writing I have usually found that the best pieces I have done have resulted not from my attempt to explain what I already know to an "unknowing" audience, but from my attempts to engage a work that I find in some way powerful even as I am unable at first to articulate just what the sources of that power might be. Writing then becomes a kind of exploration. This leads in turn to better writing, because the sense of mystery, excitement, and discovery involved in the process of exploration is never lost.

CHOOSING A WORK FROM "THE MUSEUM WITHOUT WALLS"

Writing about works of art seen in person has many advantages over writing about works one has seen only in books, but very often one has no choice. There is no substitute, for instance, for actually standing before many of David Smith's sculptures, such as *Cubi XVII* (Fig. 7), which depend for their effect on our walking around them, experiencing his work in actual space as its aspect changes from each point of view. Similarly, Courbet's giant canvasses, *A Burial at Ornans* (Fig. 8) and *The Artist's Studio* in the Musée d'Orsay, must be seen in person to be fully appreciated. Even though, in the harsh light of this particular museum, many of the details readily apparent in reproduction are virtually lost, the scale of these massive paintings, which hang over us like the rocks of Ornans in their background, can be experienced only firsthand. It is this scale, together with the tension one feels between the monumentality of the literal canvas and the triviality of the scene depicted, that provides one of the most important insights into the painting of Courbet and its influence on modern art.

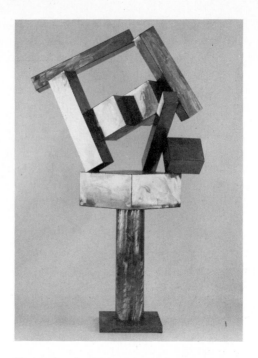

Figure 7   David Smith, *Cubi XVII*, 1963.
Polished stainless steel, 107¾ inches high by
64⅜ inches wide by 38⅛ inches deep. Courtesy The Dallas Museum of Art, The Eugene
and Margaret McDermott Fund.

But most of us are condemned to what the French writer
and novelist André Malraux called, somewhat more
optimistically, "the museum without walls." What, Malraux asks,
had the average expert on art, let alone the average citizen with
an interest in art, actually seen in the nineteenth century?

> Two or three of the great museums, and photographs, engrav-
> ings, or copies of a handful of the masterpieces of European
> art. . . . In the art knowledge of those days there existed an area
> of ambiguity: comparison of a picture in the Louvre with another
> in Madrid, in Florence, or in Rome was a comparison of a present
> vision with a memory. . . . Today, an art student can examine
> color reproductions of most of the world's great paintings and
> discover for himself a host of secondary works, as well as the
> archaic arts, the great epochs of Indian, Chinese, Japanese, and
> primitive and "folk" art. How many statues could be seen in
> reproduction in 1850? . . . A museum without walls has opened

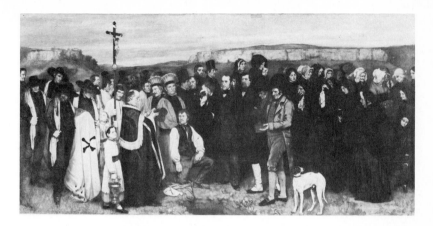

Figure 8 Gustave Courbet, *A Burial at Ornans*, 1849. Oil on canvas, 10 feet, 4 inches by 21 feet, 11 inches. Musée d'Orsay, Paris. Courtesy of the Réunion des musées nationaux.

> to us, and it will carry infinitely farther that limited revelation of the world of art which the real museums offer us within their walls.[5]

There are, then, as Malraux points out, some real advantages in having so many reproductions available on our coffee tables. It allows us at least to get a good idea of a great many of the great works of art and to see them in a larger context than would otherwise be possible. For students writing about art, however, there are a couple of important things to be aware of.

First, the quality of color reproduction varies widely, from book to book and even from image to image within a book. It is a good idea, whenever possible and especially when color is an issue that seems important to your discussion, to consult as many reproductions as you can locate (more on this is in Chapter 3, in the section on material in the library). If there seems to be some question as to which reproduction is most accurate, ask your professor for an opinion. Very often your professor will have seen the work firsthand.

Second, and this may seem obvious to some students, *never* write about a color work that you know only in black and white reproduction. Not only are you likely to make a mistake about the nature or feel of the work, but you are unable to discuss what may be one of the most important features of the work, its use of color. In Courbet's *Burial at Ornans*, for instance, a distinct positive/negative effect is created in the play of black and white between the two sides of the painting, a play accentuated by the dominance of red on the left of the canvas, especially in the beadles' dress. All this is lost in reproduction and, as a result, the unifying structure—and tension—of the painting's color scheme is lost as well.

Third, pay very close attention to the dimensions of the work, given in the caption to the reproduction (often this detail will be found only in a "List of Reproductions" in a separate section of the book). Imagine, as accurately as possible, the size of the piece with which you are dealing. Is it very small, or very large? If so, how does this alter your sense of it? It matters greatly, for instance, that you understand that Courbet's *Burial at Ornans* is over 10 feet high and nearly 22 feet long and that its figures are virtually lifesize.

Finally, recognize that even in the best reproductions you can get only the vaguest sense of a particular work's *texture*, the tactile qualities of its surface, its literal "feel." In Cubist collage, for instance, it is often impossible to tell, except in the actual presence of the work, whether a particular passage in the work is drawn, painted, or glued on. A piece of delicately grained wood might be brown paper with the grain drawn on in pencil, or it might be simulated wood-grained wallpaper pasted onto the canvas, or it might be an actual piece of wood. Such distinctions might be important in a discussion of Cubism's delight in undermining traditional notions about distinctions between the artificial and the "real."

You should approach the selection of a work to write about from a book with more or less the same degree of awareness and caution that you would employ in selecting a work to write about in a museum or gallery. In sum:

1. Determine in what ways the space of the museum or gallery (or the book) is potentially influencing your expectations. Have you come to the Guggenheim, for instance, because you want to see modern art?

2. Examine the context of the work of art that initially attracts you and determine in what ways that context informs your understanding of the work. Imagine it in some other context. Does this alter your perception of it? Are you attracted to the work despite its context or, and this is much more often the case, because of its context? Are you considering the work *as art* because you are seeing it in a museum or gallery? If you were to see Duchamp's

Fountain in a plumbing store, for instance, would you look at it as carefully as you do in the museum?

3. Have you chosen a work that is rich enough to sustain an interesting essay? Will you have enough to say?

4. Have you chosen a work that interests you? Does it seem to pose special problems? Are you surprised at your interest in it? Can you begin to articulate what is interesting about it?

5. Even if you find nothing of real interest to you, can you imagine that someone of relatively sophisticated taste and developed intelligence must find these works interesting enough for them to be on exhibit, and can you begin to determine what the source of their interest might be?

These are all questions which you need to ask yourself even before you begin to write. They will help put you in the proper spirit, that is, in a *questioning* frame of mind. Even more to the point, they are likely to help you understand your own feelings about the work before you begin to write your essay.

2

USING VISUAL INFORMATION

What to Look For
and How to Describe
What You See

Probably the greatest stumbling block for most people confronting the prospect of writing about art for the first time is what they take to be the specialized vocabulary of the connoisseur, a vocabulary with which they are not conversant. Actually, the vocabulary of good art writing is relatively simple and based on common sense. What is more esoteric and sometimes totally alien to the uninitiated is the jargon of technical and period styles that has developed as a sort of shorthand descriptive tool—a rhetoric that includes words like "classical," "baroque," "romantic," "modern," and "postmodern." If these words were not useful, they would not have the wide circulation that they do, but it is not necessary to feel comfortable with them in order to begin writing about art. They originate out of distinctions among the ways subject matter, the more common elements of form, certain principles of composition, and questions of media are employed. Most of you are quite familiar with the less specialized vocabulary—words like "line," "color," "balance," "rhythm," "sculpture," and "video," and this more usual (and useful) vocabulary is far less threatening and more accessible than concepts such as "baroque." Why do such words make a difference? Why does it matter that an artist employs line in a certain way, or that the elements in a painting repeat themselves in a visual rhythm?

It is important to point out here, again, that all art worth the name is a question of conscious choices. Given two points and the opportunity to draw a line between them, you can choose to draw a straight line, or a curved line, or a line that turns back on itself and meanders hither and thither until it finally arrives. Your choice, which may or may not be deliberate and studied, reveals a good deal about your temperament and even about the way you approach the world in general. A work of art is a compendium of such choices. Artists, who make such choices as a matter of habit and profession, make them a good deal more deliberately than you and I. This is not to say that artists necessarily think out in advance the implications of every line they make, or every application of color. Any artist will tell you that much of what they do is intuitive. However, every artist has the opportunity to revise and redo each work—and indeed very often takes advantage of that opportunity. It is probably safe to assume that what you are seeing in a work of art is an *intentional* effect, that the artist knows what he or she is doing.

What follows is a summary of the kinds of choices an artist can make. Any work of art involves *subject matter*, the *medium* in which the artist chooses to work in order to portray or express that subject matter, the particular or distinctive use of certain *formal elements* such as line and color in achieving the work, and the organization of these elements into a whole by means of what we call *principles of design* or *composition*. All of these can affect the overall *meaning* of the work—what it is capable of expressing to you, its audience. The following sections will give you some sense of the things you need to consider when you are trying to decide what a particular work of art might be about or why it might be significant or interesting. This is by no means a complete survey of the various media, principles of design, or formal elements that artists have at their disposal. It is simply an outline of why an awareness of them might help you learn to ask the right types of questions and then write a better essay. If you need more information about any given element or principle, you can consult any of the many authoritative art appreciation texts, where most of this material is treated in greater detail.

CONSIDERING
THE SUBJECT MATTER
OF THE WORK

Subject matter is the sum of the identifiable objects, incidents, and iconographic or narrative references that are recognizable in a work of art. In representational painting, these references are sometimes clear. Iconographic references are symbolic conventions that are widely recognizable in a given culture; for instance, the meaning of the cross or a crown of thorns is widely known in the Christian West. Recognition of iconographic references depends upon one's familiarity with the culture at hand. Very often simply consulting the title will make a work's range of reference more explicit. In abstract painting, however, the title may or may not help you understand the subject matter of the work. *Full Fathom Five*, the title of the Jackson Pollock painting discussed in the next chapter (Fig. 23), is very helpful indeed, but *Painting I*, the title of a Mondrian painting discussed later in this chapter (Fig. 12), is less so. Still, it is possible to say of the Mondrian that, since it announces no overt reference, its subject matter might be form itself. This is very often the case in non-representational art.

One of the most important things for you to remember when discussing subject matter is that it is in no way comparable to the *meaning* of the work. One of the classic examples of this distinction between subject matter and meaning was developed by Joshua C. Taylor in his handbook, *Learning to Look*. Taylor points out that Pietro Perugino's *Crucifixion with Saints* (Fig. 9) and Carlo Crivelli's *The Crucifixion* (Fig.10) have the same subject matter, but the meaning that subject matter assumes in each is dramatically different. For Taylor, the Perugino "would seem to quell the possible anguish and effects of suffering which might be associated with the scene and to establish a serenity and calm, a complete relaxation of the emotional and physical forces which might be expected to operate in connection with such a subject matter." In contrast, in the Crivelli there "is no rest, no calm or contemplation. Instead we take upon ourselves the anguish and physical hurt which seem to motivate the actions of the figures. And nowhere is there escape, no point on which our attention can fix itself to bring order to our excited emotions."[1] There are

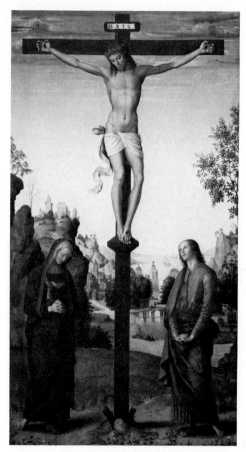

Figure 9   Pietro Perugino, *The Crucifixion with the Virgin, Saint John, Saint Jerome, and Saint Mary Magdalene* (central panel), c. 1485. Transferred from wood to canvas, 39⅞ by 22¼ inches. National Gallery of Art, Washington, D.C. Andrew W. Mellon Collection.

many structural and formal reasons for this difference—and Taylor's analysis occupies ten pages of text—but it should be sufficiently clear that whatever meaning these works possess, it is independent of subject matter. It is as if one artist sees in the scene the promise of salvation hereafter whereas the other sees the misery of our life on earth in the here and now.

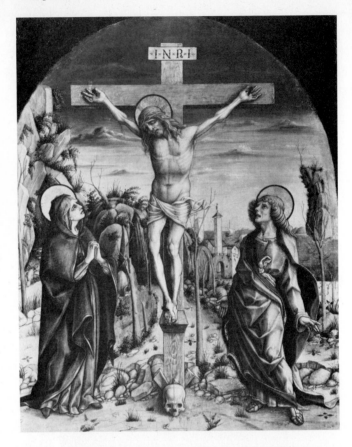

Figure 10   Carlo Crivelli, *The Crucifixion*, c. 1490. Tempera on panel, 30¹⁵⁄₁₆ by 22¾ inches. Wirt D. Walker Fund. © 1987 The Art Institute of Chicago. All rights reserved.

One of the most common mistakes student writers make is to confuse subject matter with meaning. A typical sentence describing one of these paintings might read: "Perugino [or Crivelli, take your pick] has painted a crucifixion, with all that implies." The assumption here is that the meaning of the crucifixion is clear, but such assumptions often stymie the development of ideas. The crucifixion may imply something very specific to the student writer, but Taylor's point is that the crucifixion implies something entirely different to each painter, and that implication may or may not coincide with what the writer feels about the same subject matter.

One way to assess the meaning of a given work, then, is to try to imagine other handlings of the same material. It should follow that one of the best ways to write an essay about Perugino's *Crucifixion* is to *compare* it with Crivelli's. From the differences between the two we are able to recognize some of the important decisions that Perugino made and thereby learn a great deal about his intentions.

Or imagine a painting of a red barn in a green field. What does it matter that it is bathed in sunlight? How would it look in shadow? What is the effect of its startling color contrast between red and green, and how would the same scene feel handled monochromatically as a winter scene, in the snow, at dusk? Does it matter that the barn is silhouetted against the summer sky and that your point of view is relatively low? Does it make a difference that its lines and angles are clearly delineated? Would it seem less appealing, more lonely and foreboding, if it melded into the landscape and shadows? In short, given just such a set of questions and a broad enough selection of barn paintings (and there are so many that they constitute a sort of thematic genre in American art in their own right), a reasonably significant essay on American attitudes toward landscape could probably be written. Similarly, art historians will often illustrate the difference between two stylistic periods or schools by comparing works of similar subject matter but distinctive handling. Even particular phases within an individual artist's career can be understood by means of this device. What, for instance, are the obvious differences in handling between the two versions of *Mont Sainte-Victoire* by Paul Cézanne which appear later in this chapter (Figs. 21 and 22), the second of which was painted nearly twenty years after the first? Don't you suppose that this difference tells you something about Cézanne's intentions?

Thus, while subject matter (or the lack of it, in a nonobjective painting) is the most readily apparent aspect of the work, it is also, by itself, one of the least useful in discussing the work's meaning. Rather than asking yourself what the subject matter of a particular work is, ask yourself, "What does the artist think of his or her subject matter?"

What artists think of their subject matter will be revealed in their handling of the various formal elements, the way they employ the principles of composition, and their choice of media.

DESCRIBING THE FORMAL ELEMENTS
YOU DISCOVER IN THE WORK

Line

Since line is the primary means we have for defining visual form, it stands to reason that it is one of the most important elements to be considered in preparing to write about a work of art. The difference in its use in the Perugino and Crivelli *Crucifixions* probably accounts more than anything else for the difference in meaning that we detect in these works. In the Perugino, line is determined largely by the strong vertical and horizontal axes defined by the cross itself and, working off these axes, a series of isosceles triangles, the most obvious of which is defined by the relative positions of the heads of the Virgin Mary and St. John at the two bottom corners, and Christ's head at the apex. The apex and central axis of each of the composition's other triangles remain constant, but a wider, higher triangle can be seen stretching across Christ's feet, each side defined by the trees left and right; another is defined by the outside legs of Mary and St. John, their toes pointing to the bottom corners of the triangle, and another by the almost perfectly balanced sweep of their garments across their legs. A smaller, more precise set of triangles can be seen emanating from the diamond shape of the cross at Christ's feet. Most subtle of all, this pattern is repeated in the folded fingers of both the Virgin and St. John. The cur-vilinear features of this painting, from the disposition of St. John's arms to the arched bridge in the background, seem to wrap around this triangular structure in the same manner that a circle fits neatly around an equilateral triangle.

In contrast, and although the cross divides the canvas more or less along the same geometric axis as in the Perugino, not a single line in the Crivelli seems to work in harmony with any other. If line seems to function in a more or less centripetal way in the Perugino, it is centrifugal in the Crivelli, as if erupting from the scene. Most tellingly, the painting's lines all seem to fall away from the central axis. Both the Virgin's and St. John's head tilt back rather than in toward the path of their gaze. John's hand points away from the scene. The effect is not unlike the curious sense of disorganization achieved by Courbet in his *Burial at Ornans* (Fig. 8). Despite the strong horizontal order achieved in Courbet's grouping, especially in relation to the landscape behind, and the verticality of the figures (a horizontal and vertical structure emphasized, as it often is in Western art, by the crucifix rising over the scene), Courbet fragments the composition by having each gaze—including the dog's—turn in a different direction. There is no *focus* to the scene. Implied lines of sight explode in every direction away from the supposed center of attention, the burial itself. Similarly, in the Crivelli the nervous fractures of the cliff at the painting's bottom, emphasized especially by the curved crack which seems to emanate from the skull, and the clutter of linear detail—tufts of grass here and there, tree limbs reaching every which way—all serve to create a general sense of linear disorder which stands in stark contrast to the linear regularity and harmony of the cross, let alone the balance of the Perugino.

To emphasize this difference, Taylor contrasts the treatment of St. John in both paintings. In the Crivelli, he notes:

> . . . the vertical structure-line of the figure [i.e., the fact that he is standing up in a more or less vertical way] has little meaning with regard to the effect of the whole, because the diagonal lines of his cloak are so strong that they destroy all possible sense of a vertical compact mass. And consider the nature of the lines themselves. Every curve is flattened and broken so that the line seems to struggle to reach its destination. Furthermore, if we isolate the line of the cloak, we see that far from suggesting the balanced arc of a circle, it seems rather like the lash of a whip. And this eccentric line is repeated throughout, in the robe of the Virgin, in the rocks, and even in the body of Christ. How contrasting with this is our scheme of the St. John of Perugino. The lines of the Perugino seem to wrap themselves together into a smooth-planed volume, while those of the Crivelli disperse into the air.[2]

Even more than in the figure of St. John, the difference between the two paintings is manifest in the way that each recessional plane in the Perugino is clearly outlined, the landscape receding into the distance in a reasonable and logical way, while in the Crivelli the landscape seems hopelessly confused. Notice, in the Crivelli, how the drapery on Christ's right leg sweeps in a continuous line into the landscape beyond, how the tree, which must be some distance behind him, seems to catch the drapery in the wind, and how another tree behind St. John seems to merge into the cliff across the bay. In contrast, each plane in the Perugino is distinct. Line seems to serve a regulatory function. It is as if line preserves the integrity of the space it describes, whereas in the

Crivelli it violates that integrity, disrupting our sense of organization, order, and harmony.

Shape and Space

It should be obvious, from the previous discussion, that one of the primary functions of line is to describe shape and space. One of the first questions to ask about a work of art is *how* do its lines describe shape and space? In a consistent and orderly way? Or in an apparently disruptive, even random way? One of the most powerful effects of the painting of Jackson Pollock (Fig. 1) is that its line never quite manages to define shape, let alone a consistent space. Just as it approaches the definition of a shape, it seems to break off, move in another direction. The lines of the painting seem either to pile up on one another, creating a kind of physical density and depth that seems almost galactic, or they thin out, especially at the edges, so that the painting seems flat and shallow. These are intentional effects, and they help to create a sense of ambiguity that is fundamental to Pollock's sensibility.

Normally, shape and space are defined in more consistent and accessible ways, although the lines operating to define these elements may not always be immediately obvious to you and may achieve very complicated effects. But if you learn to see these lines in the first place, and the shapes or spaces they describe, you can begin to come to grips with other, more complicated effects achieved by the artist. When you first look at Claude Monet's *Gare St. Lazare, Paris* (Fig. 11), for instance, you may not notice the diamond-shaped space that defines the center of the composition. Its top is defined by the roof of the train station, and its bottom is delineated by two implicit or *compositional lines* which meet in the hazy locomotive in the center distance and run along the tops of the two closer locomotives on each side of the station. This area is very interesting because it seems to describe both shape—a two-dimensional surface on a flat plane—and space—the airy volume of the train station itself. In fact, the bottom two lines are achieved by Monet's reference to the traditional laws of *perspective*, the geometric system of compositional lines perfected in the Renaissance for rendering the illusion of three-dimensional space. Often imaged as a road (or set of railroad tracks) disappearing into the distance, traditional

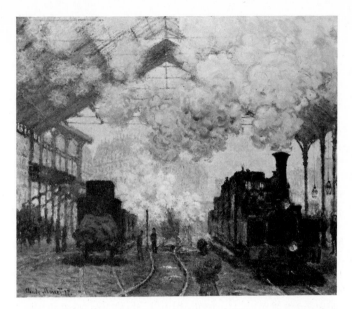

Figure 11   Claude Monet, *Gare Saint-Lazare, Paris: The Arrival of a Train*, 1877. Oil on canvas, 32¾ by 40 inches. Courtesy of The Harvard University Art Museums (Fogg Art Museum). Bequest, Collection of Maurice Wertheim, Class of 1906.

perspective is based on the observation that parallel lines seem to converge toward a common point in the distance, referred to as the *vanishing point*. In the Monet the tops (and bottoms) of the trains converge on a hypothetical vanishing point that exists directly across from our point of view, somewhere behind the distant central locomotive. The serpentine central railroad tracks would also converge on this same point if they were straightened out.

Thus the bottom of the diamond shape is composed of two lines that define three-dimensional space, while its top is composed of the two lines that define the two-dimensional edge of the roof. Monet seems to be willfully playing off the illusion of three-dimensional space against the actuality of the two-dimensional surface of the canvas (paintings, after all, are two-dimensional planes), a sense of play that the curvilinear railroad tracks emphasize since they seem to be themselves a joke on the traditional representation of the laws of perspective. Why, do you suppose, Monet would want to do this? Would it surprise you to discover that he was interested in drawing our attention not only to his choice of subject matter, but to his handling of it as well? Doesn't it make sense that he might want you to consider the surface of the canvas as a composition of effects to be enjoyed in their own right? His style of painting was as new in 1877 as the steam locomotive itself, and we move between them, subject and handling, in much the way as our eye moves between the two-dimensional design of the surface and the three-dimensional representation of space.

While Monet does not quite say that the design of the composition is more important than its subject matter, it is quite clear that, along with a number of his contemporaries, he initiates a logic that will eventually argue just that. Piet Mondrian's *Painting I* (Fig. 12), painted in 1926, almost fifty years after the Monet, has made that very step. Here the canvas is all surface; there is no illusion of depth; there is only a diamond-shaped plane, crossed by four lines, which themselves define the better part of what appears to be a square. This is a very difficult type of painting for most students to talk about because it seems to have no subject matter. If you consider, however, that one of its primary objectives might be to free the painted surface of the

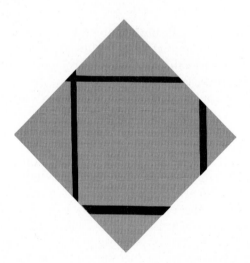

Figure 12   Piet Mondrian, *Painting, I*, 1926. Oil on canvas, diagonal measurements, 44¾ by 44 inches. Collection, The Museum of Modern Art, New York. Katherine S. Dreier Bequest.

necessity of representing three-dimensional space, then you might discover that you have something to say after all. The painting is about *form* itself.

Mondrian had, in fact, some very particular notions about the meaning of form. He believed, for instance, that the most powerful of all abstract figures was the correspondence of the vertical and the horizontal line, particularly in the right angle. He believed this convergence embodied the unity of all opposites in the universe—male and female, plus and minus, good and evil, heaven and earth, and so on. Furthermore, the diamond shape embodied the union of the three material elements—earth, air, and water—with the fourth, transcendent element—spirit.

Something like this same set of notions informs the structure of E. Fay Jones's *Thorncrown Chapel* (Fig. 13), located on a trail in the Ozark mountains near Eureka Springs, Arkansas.

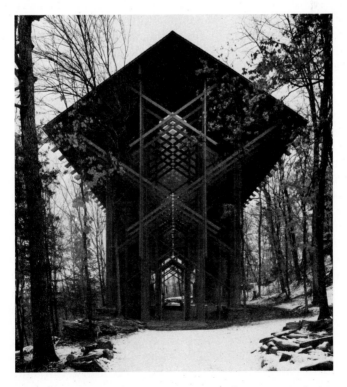

Figure 13   E. Fay Jones, *Thorncrown Chapel*, Eureka Springs, Arkansas, 1980. Photo: R. Greg Hursley.

Jones has taken the two-dimensional shape of the diamond and evoked a spatial continuity by stacking these shapes one behind the other. The *volume*, or enclosed space, thus created is reminiscent of the great Gothic cathedrals of Europe, while at the same time, because of the openness of the glass and the lightness of Jones's material, the chapel seems to blend harmoniously into the woods which surround it. The question you need to ask—a question that, even after this brief discussion, you can probably begin to answer—is what does the interplay between line, shape, and space in the Thorncrown Chapel suggest? What does it mean? What sorts of physical, and spiritual, unities does it embody?

Light and Value

In addition to the traditional systems of geometric perspective, one of the primary ways to evoke the illusion of three dimensions on a two-dimensional plane is by imitating the effects of light as it falls on three-dimensional surfaces. Gradual shifts from light areas to dark ones, across the same surface, generally indicate that you are looking at a rounded or contoured form. Edward Weston's photograph *Bell Pepper #30* (Fig. 14) is an almost classic example of this modulation. It is as if every contour of the pepper, every inundation and hollow, has been made visible by Weston. One of the most powerful effects of this photograph, in fact, is the implicit analogy Weston draws between the formal contours of the pepper and those of the human body. We might be gazing at a seated nude whose back is to us, her right arm over her head, her left hand caressing the back of her neck, and her knees drawn up to her chest. These are the same shifts and gradations in value that we recognize in the form of representation in painting and drawing known as *chiaroscuro*. In Italian, *chiaroscuro* means light (*chiaro*) to dark (*oscuro*)—and notice how language here reflects technique, as the end of the first word melds into the beginning of the second. The technique is evidenced in the drawing by Charles Sheeler (Fig. 15). It is hardly accidental that Sheeler's photography is held in as high esteem as his painting and drawing. Both the photographer and the painter are interested in the same thing— the revelation of form, and sensuous form at that, through the gradual modulation of tonal value.

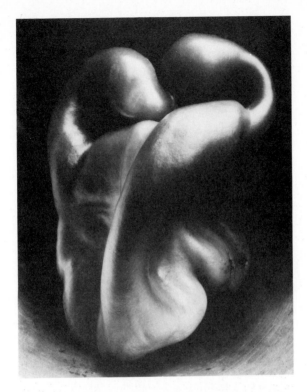

Figure 14   Edward Weston, *Bell Pepper #30.* © 1981
Arizona Board of Regents, Center for Creative
Photography.

Photography, in fact, literally means "drawing with light,"
and it is intimately concerned with rendering the three-dimensional world in two dimensions, by means of light. Alfred
Stieglitz's *Hand of Man* (Fig. 16) recalls in many ways, and probably intentionally, Claude Monet's *Gare St. Lazare* (Fig. 11). The
Impressionists, too, were interested in rendering the effects of
light. Yet Stieglitz's photograph, for all its hazy atmospherics, is
different in feel from Monet's painting. How can we account for
this difference?

It is not so much a question of color versus black and
white—although that enters into it, since the Monet maintains a
fairly uniform "blue" effect throughout—but more a question of
value. Despite the fact that there is great tonal contrast between
the black engines in the Monet and the lighter tonal values above

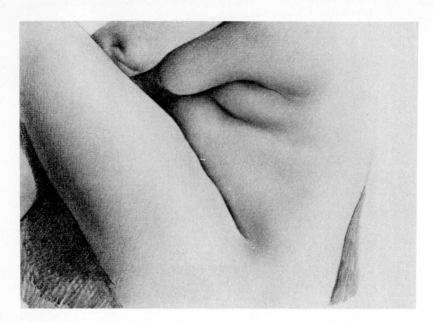

Figure 15   Charles Sheeler, *Nude Torso*. Pencil on ivory wove paper, 11.5 by 16 cm. Gift of Friends of American Art. © 1987 The Art Institute of Chicago. All rights reserved.

them, the painting maintains a logical tonal consistency, moving from dark to light as we move from the foreground into recessional space, from inside to outside. Stieglitz's photograph, on the other hand, is alternately clear and hazy, brightly white and deeply black, at every level. The linear clarity of the tracks is contrasted with the amorphous bellows of the engine, the bright sky with the deeply shadowed foreground.

Such strong value contrasts contribute greatly to a sense of drama and tension in a work of art. In terms of the Stieglitz photograph, the title becomes ambiguous by force of the contrasts apparent in the work itself. The "hand of man" seems to have contributed a certain clarity and direction to the scene—witness the tracks—and yet simultaneously an amorphous confusion. This double sense of things, this tension between order and chaos, is embodied in the contrast between light and dark in the photograph itself. Minimal value contrasts often have the opposite effect. A work of art that seems uniform in value, such as Perugino's *Crucifixion*, usually evokes feelings of calm and harmony.

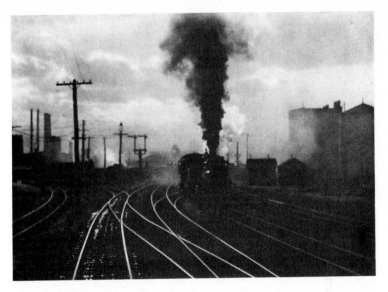

Figure 16   Alfred Stieglitz, *Hand of Man*, 1902. Philadelphia Museum of Art, Dorothy Norman Collection.

Color

Though it is easier to think of questions of value in terms of black and white, the same rules apply to color as well. Think, for instance, of the difference in value between pink and maroon: one is red saturated with white and the other is red saturated with black. When we refer to someone who wears a lot of pastels, we mean someone who dresses in colors light in tone. It is not hard to imagine a painting of a red ball that moves in value from a white highlight to a black shadow through all the various tints and shades of red (the color that results from adding white to a pure hue is called a *tint* of that hue, and the color that results from adding black to the hue is called a *shade*).

Yet color functions in works of art in terms more complicated than just those of value. In fact, in the same way that black and white can be considered opposites, each color has its opposite number as well. These opposites are called *complementary* colors (spelled with *e* not *i*—one of the most common spelling mistakes made in art writing). Complements are pairs of colors which, when mixed together in almost equal proportion, create neutral grays, but which when standing side by side, as pure hues, seem to intensify and even contradict one another.

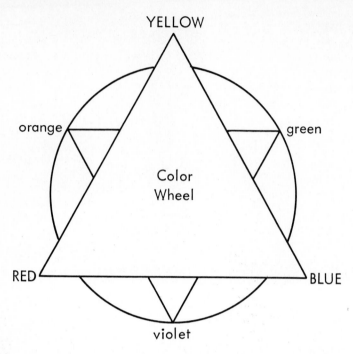

The traditional color wheel, above, makes these oppositions clear.

Each *primary* color—red, blue, and yellow—has, as its complement, a *secondary* color—green, orange, and violet, respectively. Thus the standard complementary pairs are red/green, blue/orange, and yellow/violet (and, obviously, the intermediate hues have complementary opposites as well—the complement of red-orange is blue-green, for instance). Furthermore, just as gray moderates between black and white—as white becomes gray with the addition of black and vice versa—each color gradually moderates into the hue of its neighbor with the addition of its neighbor. Thus the more yellow one adds to green, for instance, the more yellow-green the color becomes. Neighboring colors on the color wheel are called *analogous* colors. Unlike complementary pairs which create a sense of contradiction or opposition against each other, analogous pairs usually seem to rest harmoniously beside each other. The analogous blue-green relationships are commonly referred to as *cool*, and red-orange combinations are said to be *warm*, or even hot.

Color theory is a vastly complicated field—one that is hardly settled, even among physicists—and the scheme described above is a vast oversimplification of the ways in which colors interact. Nevertheless, in writing about art it is important to understand these complementary and analogous groupings because a great many works depend upon them to some degree in order to achieve their effects. Much of the power of the painting of Vincent Van Gogh, for instance, depends upon his use of complementary color schemes. In a letter to his brother Theo, he described his famous painting *The Night Café* (Fig. 17) in these terms:

> In my picture of the "Night Café" I have tried to express the idea that the café is a place where one can ruin oneself, run mad, or commit a crime. I have tried to express the terrible passions of humanity by means of red and green. The room is blood-red and dark yellow, with a green billiard table in the middle; there are four lemon-yellow lamps with a glow of orange and green. Everywhere there is a clash and contrast of the most alien reds and greens in the figures of little sleeping hooligans in the empty dreary room, in violet and blue. The white coat of the patron, on vigil in a corner, turns lemon-yellow, or pale luminous green.

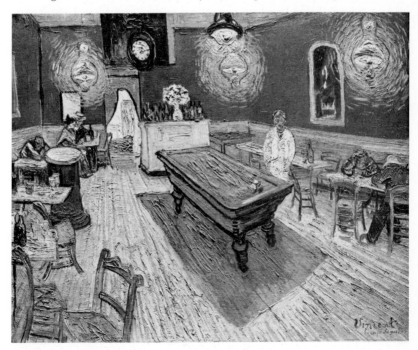

Figure 17   Vincent Van Gogh, *The Night Café*, 1888. Oil on canvas, 28½ by 36¼ inches. Yale University Art Gallery, Bequest of Stephen Carlton Clark.

> So I have tried to express, as it were, the powers of darkness in a low wine-shop, and all this in an atmosphere like a devil's furnace of pale sulphur. . . . It is color not locally true from the point of view of the stereoscopic realist, but color to suggest the emotion of an ardent temperament.[3]

The color scheme, especially the contrast between the complements red and green, is meant to suggest the tension of the scene, the sense that beneath the surface an almost violent energy or fury is about to erupt. Things do not go together here, either literally or pictorially.

In a painting such as Matisse's *Decorative Figure on an Ornamental Background* (reproduced on the back cover) many of these complementary contrasts are employed. Complementary contrasts between orange and blue can be seen throughout the pattern on the back wall, and between red and green in the painting's many flower patterns. Even the *intensity* of the colors—that is, their relative purity of hue—seems willfully arbitrary: compare, for instance, the dull reds and greens of the carpet with the brightness of the lemons, their blue-green bowl, and many of the painting's various tints of blue. Yet surprisingly, the painting seems overall to be unified in effect. The tension that we felt in the Van Gogh is absent in the Matisse.

This is surely a result, in part, of Matisse's subject matter. It is also so because, in various ways, he is trying to make contrasting elements work together in harmony. Like Van Gogh, he is not interested in representing the precise color of a thing. The Impressionists had freed painting of the necessity of representing *local* color (that is, the color we "know" a thing to be in the sense that we "know" trees are green) and chose to represent the *optical* color of what they saw (in the sense that a hill covered with "green" trees will often appear blue). Matisse and Van Gogh have gone even further. "I use color," Matisse would say, "as a means of expressing my emotion, and not for transcribing nature."[4] As opposed to Van Gogh's, however, Matisse's emotions generally run toward the luxurious, the calm, and the sensuous. This feeling is, in fact, something of which even Van Gogh dreamed. In the same letter to his brother Theo in which he described the color effects of *The Night Café*, he claimed that he was always in hope of expressing "the love of two lovers by a marriage of two complementary colors, their mingling and their opposition, the mysterious vibrations of kindred tones."[5] One senses, in Matisse's *Decorative Figure*, that so many different and opposing colors have been employed in order to create a visual feast for the eye, to surround, even embrace the viewer with color. It is as if the painting resolves opposition.

It should be clear, even from this brief discussion, that different artists use color in different ways. Yellow may be "sulphurous" or "urinous" in one context, while it may shine like lemons or gold in another. Combinations of complementary colors may create tension in a painting, or they may be harmonized. Analogous color schemes often create a unified effect, but just as often that sense of unity can transform itself into a feeling of monotony. Meaningful discussions of an artist's use of color must often rely on a context greater than the individual work— as I have relied on the artists' own words here in order to help us understand their different intentions.

As a writer, you must always be aware of the fact that the associations you have with a particular color are not universal. If you hear, "red," you may think "roses" and "love" while the next person thinks "blood," and the next person thinks "communism." Whatever you have to say about color is best said in the context of other parts of your discussion. If Van Gogh's lines seem violent and disruptive, for instance, this impression would support your notion that he is employing complementary colors in order to create a sense of disunity and impending chaos. Ask yourself, how does the artist employ color and what does it mean? *But then ask yourself*, do other things about the composition support this reading?

Other Elements

There are a number of other formal elements that might be important for you to consider. What, for instance, is the *texture* of the work? If it is uniformly smooth, does this smoothness contribute to a sense of harmony? Consider Van Gogh's *Night Café* again. Doesn't the thickness of his brushstroke, its very assertive and gestural presence, assert his involvement in the depiction of what you see? Doesn't it invoke expressivity? David Smith's *Cubi* (Fig. 7) are distinguished by the high-tech, geometric feel of their stainless steel construction which is opposed to the rough, gestural polishing which Smith employs on their surface, giving them almost the feeling of being handmade, certainly establishing a certain sense of Smith's intimacy with them.

The markings on Smith's sculpture in fact invoke another formal element, one that we often tend to disregard in relation to most media in the arts—that is, *time*. Smith's *Cubi*, which were designed to be placed outdoors, in the landscape, reflect the most subtle changes in light, hour by hour and season to season. Just as our conception of them changes according to *where* we put ourselves in relation to them, it also changes according to *when* we see them. The result is that his sculptures feel dynamic rather than static, active rather than passive.

Similarly, Michael Heizer's *Complex One/City* (Fig. 18) is a pyramid-like mound 140 feet long and 24 feet high, made of compacted earth in the desert of Nevada. From directly in front of it, at a distance of at least half a mile, it appears as if this construction is a rectangular plane, framed by a border of dark concrete with a sort of slash down the middle. As one approaches it, the frame begins to fragment (Fig. 19)—its apparently continuous line is actually composed of several distinct sections placed at differing intervals both from the mound and from one another. Furthermore, the mound, which seems ver-

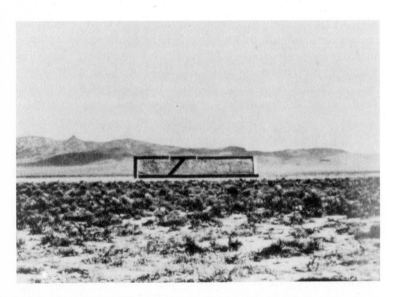

Figure 18   Michael Heizer, *Complex One/City*, 1972–76. Concrete, steel, and compacted earth, 110 by 140 by 23½ feet. Collection of Virginia Dawn and the artist. Location: Central Eastern Nevada.

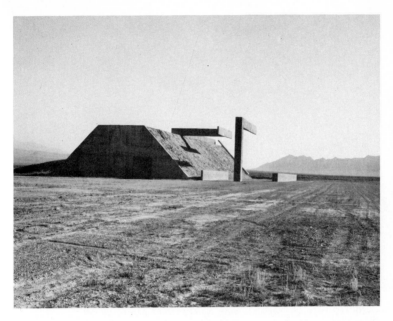

Figure 19   Michael Heizer, *Complex One/City*, second view.

tical from a distance, reveals itself to be sloped. The piece itself remains static, but it changes according to one's own movement in time and space.

With the invention of photography in the last century, time entered the domain of art in radically new terms. Photography seems to convey the essence of a particular time and place, and this aura of authenticity, together with its sense of instantaneous vision, of the moment itself captured forever, constitutes a large part of its appeal. Today it is apparent that the dialogue between the present moment of our seeing the photograph—our actual experience of it in "real" time, versus the way in which the photograph seems to embody, or make present, something long lost or far away, has revolutionized our sense of time and space. The "museum without walls," discussed in the last chapter, is a perfect example. The reproductions in this book constitute the small collection of a "museum without walls" in its own right, and a very good example of how this museum operates is your relation to the photographs of Michael Heizer's *Complex One/City*. Most of you will never see it, but you "know" it through the

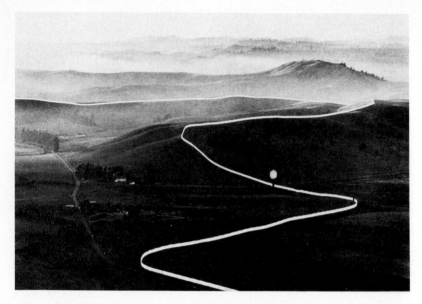

Figure 20   Christo, *Running Fence, Sonoma and Marin Counties, California,* 1972–76. © Christo 1976. Photo: Gianfranco Gorgoni.

photographs. Many contemporary artists construct works which most of us will never know except through their photographic documentation. Christo's *Running Fence* (Fig. 20) was constructed in California in 1976. It was composed of an 18-foot high nylon fence which ran 24½ miles through farmland in Sonoma County. The fence was up for only two weeks in September, and then it was dismantled. What is the work of art? The photograph of it—and other documentation like it—or the original project? Is there an easy answer to this question?

You need only consider your own relation to a photograph of yourself taken as a child. It is you, and it isn't, and whatever difference and similarity you can see or feel is a question of time. The photograph seems to transcend time, in other words, even as it submits everything to time's scrutiny. It is even worth suggesting that today we determine similarity and difference—the idea of change itself—in photographic terms.

One of the best summaries of our relation to photography is a provocative and reasonably accessible set of essays by Susan Sontag, originally written for *The New York Review of Books* and collected under the title *On Photography*.[6] Anyone interested in pursuing the implications of the medium should begin there. But two other media—video and film—have an even greater reliance on time. One of the traditional distinctions among the arts has been that the plastic arts—painting, drawing, and sculpture—are *spatial* media, while the other arts—dance, music, literature—are primarily *temporal* in nature. Video and film seem to be somehow both.

Most of us think of video in relation to commercial television. However, many video artists purposefully manipulate the medium in order to distinguish what they do from the television we habitually consume. The most common difference, again, is the medium's relation to time. Standard television time is based upon the length of the commercial—10, 30, 60, and, less commonly, 120 seconds in duration. As David Antin has pointed out in a detailed analysis of the medium, there is really no difference between commercial time and the structure of time in television programs generally. A news "story," for instance, generally fits into this same time scheme, and a baseball game is a succession of pitches, hits, and catches that fit the same pace.[7] Video artists often ignore this pace completely, so to a viewer expecting "television," the work usually seems boring. Very commonly, the camera is held in one position, for as long as an hour. As a result, one can, if one gives the medium its due, pay close attention to other of its aspects that we generally ignore, such as the peculiar way that it represents and distorts deep space.

Perhaps one of the best ways to think of film, which can reproduce space in ways far more sophisticated than can video, is as an assemblage of various spatial and temporal points of view. The fade-in and fade-out, flashback and flashforward, closeup and longshot, and even the multi-image screen, all combine to produce film's many, sometimes startling visual effects. This multiplicity of visual techniques combines with the more purely temporal means of narrative, dialogue, and musical score to create one of the most complex of the arts. Many contemporary artists have used film as a way to document the production of their works. Christo, for instance, makes films of all his projects, films that survive the work of art itself. Thus the film has a curious temporal relation to the actual work that is not unlike the relation of the photograph to its subject matter.

RECOGNIZING
THE PRINCIPLES
OF DESIGN

Rhythm and Repetition

One thing that would suggest that the traditional distinction between spatial and temporal media might not be altogether valid is the sense of visual rhythm and repetition we often experience before works of art in which certain formal elements recur, in either exact of analogous terms. The analogy to the temporal experience of musical rhythm seems reasonably precise, especially when we recognize that in both music and the plastic arts—to say nothing of poetry—rhythm and repetition serve to organize, or order, the work into distinct and recognizable patterns.

Perhaps the most common source of this sense of rhythm and repetition in art derives from the way in whch the artist manipulates line and shape. Cézanne's *Mont Sainte-Victoire* (Fig.

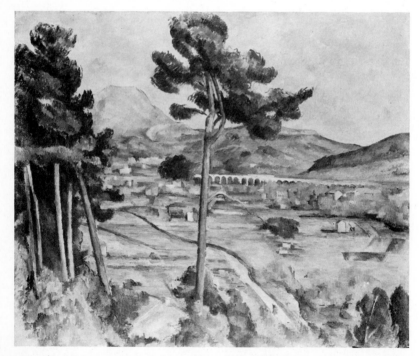

Figure 21   Paul Cézanne, *Mont Sainte-Victoire*, 1885–87. Oil on canvas, 25¾ by 32⅛ inches. The Metropolitan Museum of Art, Bequest of Mrs. H. O. Havemeyer, 1929.

21), for instance, is composed of a number of repeated shapes and lines which serve to unify the composition. Notice that the slope of the mountain itself is repeated down the right edge of the top of the central tree, again with uncanny accuracy in the branch that extends from the right side of the tree halfway down its trunk, and again, immediately below that, in the large curve of the river. The shape of the river on the left of the tree seems to echo, in reverse, the hill that comes into the composition from the right. A rhythm of arches extends the length of the railroad viaduct, and throughout the painting, small, square, and rectangular areas—buildings, roofs, chimneys, fields—echo and repeat each other's shapes. In a later version of this same motif (Fig. 22), the precise elements of the landscape have virtually disappeared, yet here the small quadrilateral shapes—which now seem to have been created by single brushstrokes, moving in a sort of pulse through the composition—ascend toward the top of the mountain in a rhythm and movement of growing clarity and definition finally achieved by Cézanne at the painting's (and the mountain's) summit.

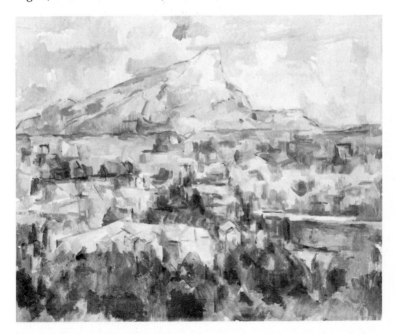

Figure 22   Paul Cézanne, *Mont Sainte-Victoire*, 1904–06. Oil on canvas, 27⅞ by 36⅛ inches. Philadelphia Museum of Art, George W. Elkins Collection.

Matisse's *Decorative Figure* (back cover) engages the repetition of pattern and design as a major theme, in the way that wallpaper, for instance, is decorative in the harmonious repetition and movement of its elements. There are many other more subtle repetitions of shape, however, both implied and overt, which serve to unify this composition. Notice, for instance, the way that many of the forms here are circular or ovoid in structure—the top of the planter, the bowl, the lemons, the breasts and belly of the nude, the sweeping curve of the drapery which covers her, many of the shapes in the wallpaper, and the patterns on the carpet. Counterpointed to this circular rhythm is a more geometric design, into whch the nude's back and lower leg seem forcefully inserted and which is composed additionally of the square shape in the lower right-hand corner, the stripes in the carpet, and the mirror behind her head. This more geometric pattern corresponds, of course, to one of the design elements of painting that we most commonly ignore—the frame itself with its insistent vertical and horizontal format. But notice how Matisse creates a series of right triangles with the frame as the right angle and with each stripe on the carpet as a hypotenuse. Notice further how the nude reflects this same structure in reverse, her back and left leg forming the right angle and her raised right leg forming the hypotenuse. Since decoration usually draws attention to the planarity of the composition and creates a sense of movement between and among its elements, the repetitions of line and shape in *Decorative Figure* help to create a sense of overall unity and composition and, simultaneously, a feeling of visual variety and multiplicity.

Balance

If you compare Cézanne's 1885–87 version *Mont Sainte-Victoire* (Fig. 21) to Perugino's *Crucifixion* (Fig. 9), you will notice that one thing these very different paintings have in common is that they can be divided into more or less equal quarters across the axis formed, in the Cézanne, by the central vertical tree and the arched railroad bridge and, in the Perugino, along the vertical axis of the cross and the horizon line. This geometric division, which again echoes and reinforces the shape of the frame in each painting, creates a sense of symmetry and equilibrium in both compositions. The sense of disequilibrium and chaos apparent in the Crivelli *Crucifixion* (Fig. 10) derives in large part from the fact that, despite its overall symmetry and balance on a vertical axis, created by both the cross and the overriding arch, there is no clear horizontal symmetry, and the structure of the right side of the composition seems radically different from the structure of the left. It is as if Crivelli has purposely defied our expectation of balance.

There are many other ways to achieve a sense of balance in a composition. *Radial balance* is created when all the elements of the composition seem to emerge from a real or actual focal point. In an *asymmetrically balanced* composition, a perceived center of gravity seems to balance elements. It is like balancing a teeter-totter with a very heavy child on one side and a light child on the other: the heavy child must move toward the center of the teeter-totter while the lighter child sits on the very end. In a composition that is asymmetrically balanced, visually "heavy" elements—they can seem heavy because of their relatively large size or because of their relative darkness of tone and color—occur toward the center of the work while "lighter" elements move toward the opposite side. In Piet Mondrian's *Painting I* (Fig. 12), for instance, the lines on the right and bottom sides of the composition are wider than the lines on the left and top, and as a result, Mondrian balances the central square in the diamond shape by moving it to the right, so that *more* of the square is visible on the left.

Proportion

Proportion is the relationship of each part of the composition to the whole and to each other part. An excellent example of its use can be seen in the 1904–06 version of *Mont Sainte-Victoire* (Fig. 22). You will notice that the composition is divided neatly at the foot of the mountain. This line, with the mountain and clouds above it and the countryside of Aix-en-Provence in Southern France below it, very closely corresponds to what the ancient Greeks referred to as "the golden section." This proportion—which is found, incidentally, in living organisms—can be defined mathematically as follows: the smaller section (in the Cézanne, the area above the line running across the bottom of the mountain) is to the larger section (the countryside below) as the larger section is to the whole painting. In numbers, each ratio is 1 to 1.618. Not only did the Greeks use this "ideal" or "perfect" proportion as the basis for constructing their greatest buildings, but they conceived of the human body in the same terms. The perfect body, they reasoned, consisted of a torso and head roughly equivalent to the vertical height of the top of the Cézanne composition, the body from the waist down equivalent to the lower part of the composition. Such proportional ideals, it is worth suggesting, dominate our visual thinking to this day—from our sense of when a landscape painting "feels" right to our sense of the ideal human body.

Scale

Scale is an issue with which we have dealt already in relation to the "museum without walls." It is sometimes very difficult, for instance, to get an accurate feeling for a work of art's size from a photograph of it. To get a sense of this principle, you need only think again of the actual size of the Courbet *Burial at Ornans* (Fig. 8) and the viewer's inability to take it all in at once, compared with the sense of containment one feels before it in reproduction. Similarly, only from a series of photographs or the film can you get any sense at all of the enormity of Christo's *Running Fence* (Fig. 20). But to experience the fence itself was to get a far different sense of scale than even the photographs or the film can elicit. For the few days it was up, running up and down hills, along valleys and ridges, from horizon to horizon across nearly 25 miles of landscape, the fence articulated the immensity of the Northern California panorama like nothing before or after it has ever done. It seemed, in fact, to elongate space, to stretch out the scene.

Other, more subtle effects can be achieved by manipulating scale. In Cézanne's 1885–87 *Mont Sainte-Victoire,* for instance, there appears to be a large bush or tree at the end of the railroad viaduct just to the left of the central tree. If it were really a tree, however, it would be 300 or 400 feet tall. It is, in fact, part of the pine in the foreground. In a very subtle move here, Cézanne purposefully draws the most distant planes of the canvas up to the closest by confusing our reading of what is near and what is far away. As a result, our attention is drawn to the surface of the composition, to its organization as a design, as much as to its representation of a three-dimensional world.

Unity and Variety

One of the primary sources of interest and power in many works of art is the way their various elements are combined to create a sense of oneness or unity. Frank Lloyd Wright's Guggenheim Museum (Fig. 5) is a case in point. What has startled museum-goers even to the present day is the way in which its interior spiral walkway fits into the primarily vertical and horizontal architecture of the building itself and the city as a whole. Furthermore, as one views works of art in this space, the vertical and horizontal frames of the paintings would seem, intellectually, to be at odds with the slope of the ramp, and yet, by means of subtle shifts in elevation, these contrasting elements seem to work together rather than in opposition. Similarly, part of the enormous visual power of Matisse's *Decorative Figure on an Ornamental Background* is the way in which its curvilinear elements harmonize with its more rectilinear ones. "For me," Matisse would say, "the subject of the painting and the background of the painting have the same value, or, to put it more clearly, no point is more important than any other, all that counts is the composition."[8] Straight line and curve, figure and ground, even the complementary color scheme, all these elements are combined to create an overall design and pattern that seems balanced and harmonious. According to Matisse again, "The colors, the lines, are the forces, and in the play of these forces, in their equilibrium, resides the secret of creation."[9]

CONSIDERING QUESTIONS OF MEDIUM

This is not the place to discuss the various capabilities and advantages (or disadvantages) of the specific media—painting, printmaking, drawing, sculpture, architecture, photography, video, film, fiber, ceramics, metal, and glass. Each has its distinctive features, and within each there are various subcategories—in painting, for instance, there is oil, acrylic, watercolor, tempera, and so on—which can elicit far different effects in themselves. You do need to keep in mind, however, the important differences between the two-dimensional media, the three-dimensional media, and those newer forms which combine the spatial sense of the plastic arts with the temporal forms of the other arts (i.e., video, film, and to some extent photography). These distinctions have already been brought to your attention. Nevertheless, if you feel you are looking at a work that seems informed particularly by the choice of material, then by all means learn what that choice of material entails and implies. Doing so may involve a little research, or a few well-placed questions, but trust your instincts and follow up hunches like this. The ability of acrylic paints to act in solution more or less like watercolors, for instance, allowed abstract painters in the late 1950s to achieve certain stain techniques on canvas that had never really been possible before. Similarly, Frank Lloyd Wright's architectural achievements are firmly rooted in the invention, at the turn of the last century, of steel beam and reinforced concrete construction techniques.

You need to pay especially close attention to questions of media when they seem, in one way or another, to be combined in a single work. What is Christo's *Running Fence*, for instance? Is it a piece of sculpture, or is it landscape architecture? Is it film, or is it photography? Or, even, is it public relations? And what do these things have to do with one another? Michael Heizer's *Complex One/City* seems, from a distance, to be a kind of painting, then, closer in, a sort of architecture, perhaps a building or temple, and then, when it reveals itself to be impenetrable, a large-scale sculpture. It articulates primarily the limitations of each of these different media: one's inability to get "close" to painting, the seeming necessity for architecture to be functional or useful, or, conversely, the fact that sculpture is in the end not a very useful allocation of space—monolithic and cold, it is as uninhabitable as the desert itself.

ASKING YOURSELF ABOUT THE WORK OF ART: A SUMMARY

The following set of questions derives from the previous discussion and is meant as a quick reminder of the kinds of things you might ask yourself about a work of art. It is by no means complete, and you almost surely will discover that most works of art raise other questions as well. Nor will every question be of particular importance in your coming to terms with each work you see. Still, it does provide you with a model of the kind of analytic process which will help you understand what you see.

One last word of warning: Don't take these questions as an outline of your eventual paper. Good papers are never written by answering a series of predetermined questions. Consider them, rather, as a guide designed to help you take the notes that will eventually lead to that good paper.

1. Determine what the subject matter of the work is:

   What is its title? Does the title help you interpret what you see? Can you imagine different treatments of the same subject matter that would change the way you read the work?

2. Consider the formal elements of the work and how they relate to its subject matter:

   How is line employed in the work? Does it seems to regulate or order the composition? Does it seem to fragment the work? Is it consistent with traditional laws of perspective or does it violate them?

   What is the relation of shape to space in the work?

   How do light and value function in the work? Is there a great deal of tonal contrast, or it is held to a minimum?

   What is the predominant color scheme of the work? Are complementary or analogous colors employed?

   What other elements seem important? Is your attention drawn to the work's texture? Does time seem an important factor in your experience of the work?

3. Then ask yourself how these elements are organized:

   Is there significant use of visual rhythm and repetition of elements?

   Is the composition balanced? Symmetrically? Asymmetrically?

   Do various elements seem proportional, and how does the question of scale affect your perception?

   Does the composition seem unified or not?

4. Next consider how the artist's choice of medium has played a role in the presentation of the various elements and their organization or design:

   Are effects achieved that are realizable only in this particular medium? If more than one medium is involved, what is their relation?

5. Finally, consider what all this might *mean*:

   What is the artist trying to say about the subject matter of the work? What feelings or attitudes does the composition seem to evoke, and what specific elements or design choices in the composition account for these feelings?

3

RESPONDING TO THE VERBAL FRAME:
Where Else to Look for Help in Understanding What You See

TAKING THE TITLE AND LABEL INTO ACCOUNT

On the third floor of the Museum of Modern Art in New York City, in one of the first of the galleries dedicated to contemporary art, a comparatively small, dark green oil painting by Jackson Pollock (Fig. 23) is sometimes on display. It is, at first glance, not nearly as engaging as some of the larger works by Pollock or his Abstract Expressionist colleagues that occupy most of the later rooms. It lacks their scale—which is to say, their presence—and, given the more or less ominous and dense tone of the composition, quite apparently their visual variety and interest. It is not particularly well lit, nor is it placed on the wall in such a way that your attention is immediately drawn to it. You assume, rather, that it is placed here as a kind of antecedent to the later, greater works to follow.

However, it is a very interesting painting, which you might discover if you have the time and the inclination, and if you take the opportunity to stroll up to it and read its title: *Full Fathom Five*. This title immediately tells something very specific to someone familiar with Shakespeare. But even to someone for whom the phrase is unfamiliar, a certain resonance immediately develops that alters one's sense of the painting. You might know only that the word "fathom" is a nautical measure of depth, but suddenly, when you look back at the canvas, at its deep green recesses, you are underwater.

The title is the first verbal clue that you are given about the meaning of the work. It never ceases to astonish me how often students simply ignore the title in their discussion of a work of art. A colleague of mine once had a student who began an essay on Marcel Duchamp's *Nude Descending a Staircase* by writing, "In this painting Duchamp depicts a person going up the stairs." This is a particularly vivid example of a quite common occur-

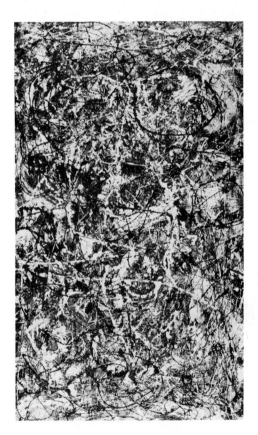

Figure 23 Jackson Pollock, *Full Fathom Five*, 1947. Oil on canvas, with nails, tacks, buttons, key, coins, cigarettes, matches, etc., 50⅞ by 30⅛ inches. Collection, The Museum of Modern Art, New York. Gift of Peggy Guggenheim.

rence. The title, in fact, is one of the first pieces of information you must take into account. It is sometimes of no apparent help whatever, but even in that case you can surely recognize that, for whatever reasons (reasons that you need to begin to figure out, incidentally), the artist has chosen not to help you, or has decided to confuse you. Not long after Pollock painted *Full Fathom Five*, he stopped naming his paintings and started numbering them. In a 1950 interview with Pollock and his wife Lee Krasner for *The New Yorker*, Krasner explained: "Numbers are neutral. They make people look at a picture for what it is—pure painting." Pollock then clarified her point: "I decided to stop adding to the confusion. . . . Abstract painting is abstract. It confronts you."[1] You may feel, in the case of *Full Fathom Five*, that the title does indeed add to the confusion. You probably will know that it's a quotation, but you may not recognize that it's from Shakespeare, let alone which play (more than one student has assumed that it's a reference to Jules Verne's *20 Thousand Leagues Under the Sea*). Nevertheless, it is worth suggesting that the difference between *Full Fathom Five* and some of the later, numbered Pollock paintings is that the former doesn't confront you in the way that a painting like *Number 1, 1948* (Fig. 1) does. The scale of the two paintings is dramatically different. *Number 1, 1948* is 5 feet 8 inches high and 8 feet 8 inches long. It literally surrounds you. *Full Fathom Five* is a comparatively small, rather unassuming, dark painting. It needs its title.

When you encounter a title you don't understand, ask somebody if they recognize what it refers to. Or consult *Bartlett's Dictionary of Quotations*. The multi-volume *Oxford English Dictionary*, although intimidating-looking, can be particularly useful for old-fashioned and archaic meanings, since each entry consists of a history, with example, of the various usages any given word has undergone. Whenever there's a word in a title that you don't understand, look it up. Sooner or later, the reference will usually come clear. Occasionally, it is even beneficial to look up a word you think you do understand. The contemporary abstract painter Robert Motherwell entitled a group of his paintings the *Open* series because the word "open," which seems simple enough, is actually extremely rich in meaning.

The reference, in the case of the Pollock painting, is to Shakespeare's play *The Tempest* (even the title of this play seems to resonate in the dark swirl of Pollock's canvas). Early in the play, Ariel, an "airy spirit," as Shakespeare calls him, sings this song to Ferdinand, the son of the King of Naples, who has just come ashore after a shipwreck in which, he believes, he has lost his father. The song leads him to believe that the island is somehow magical:

> *Full fathom five thy father lies;*
> *Of his bones are coral made;*
> *Those are pearls that were his eyes;*
> *Nothing of him that doth fade*
> *But doth suffer a sea-change*
> *Into something rich and strange.*
>
> *(Tempest,* I, ii)

Now these are words that clearly help you understand the painting. Pollock has led you in their direction, and he intends for you to consider them. They *frame* the painting in a way you cannot afford to ignore.

What they suggest, first of all, is that some sort of "sea-change" has occurred in the painting which has transformed its elements into something "rich and strange." By now you should know to ask yourself, "Well, what are the elements of this painting?" Is there anything special about them? Again, if you were to go back to the label accompanying the Pollock painting, to the verbal frame, you would find some additional help. In its entirety it reads: "Jackson Pollock. *Full Fathom Five*, 1947. Oil on canvas, with nails, tacks, buttons, key, coins, cigarettes, matches, etc., 50 7/8 x 30 1/8 in." You go back to the painting and consider it more closely, looking to see if you can detect this accumulation of material in it. And of course you can: There are all manner of things buried in the paint, held in place by the sweep and swirl of Pollock's line. Here's a coin, a nail, a screw, a comb, and there's the key—the key to what? you wonder.

Inevitably, the thought arises that these "things" have been transformed—"suffered a sea-change"—into this "painting," a painting which Pollock has implicitly characterized as "rich and strange." Taken together, the elements of the verbal frame, as we have so far established it, can help us begin to understand the exact nature of this transformation. We have moved from the recognizable and the commonplace—the world of nails, coins, and combs—to the virtually unrecognizable and the "strange" world of the painting itself—and if this painting seems strange to you now, imagine how it must have appeared in 1947. The agent of this change seems, in fact, to be painting—more precisely, the act of painting—which has worked on the elements lying on its "ground" in a manner analogous to the sea, covering them, burying them beneath the sand, uncovering them again. If the gestural sweep of Pollock's line can be defined at all, then perhaps comparing it to the ebb and eddy, the churn and whirl, of sea and tempest is as close as one can come. Most important, the title announces that the painting is as much a burial as it is a transformation. Whatever riches it may contain, they lay "full fathom five" below. Nothing in Pollock's entire *oeuvre* (that is, the body of his work) better defines the sense of space one feels before his canvases. One peers deep into this work, and it is dark down below. A few things are visible, hinting at more. But Pollock has buried them forever, beneath the swirl of his paint, and they will never be seen again. Pollock gives you a surface, like the surface of the sea, which you know conceals more than it reveals. He provides you with an unfathomable mystery.

CONSIDERING INFORMATIONAL LABELS ACCOMPANYING THE WORK

Though the Pollock painting in the Museum of Modern Art is not accompanied by any more information than I have already given you, it should not be hard to imagine how more information on the label might help you to come to grips with the painting. A simple citation of the appropriate passage in Shakespeare would be helpful to most people. Many museums do provide this sort of informational label as a matter of course.

Most people spend at least as much time reading informational labels in museums as they do looking at the art works themselves (and this is not the least reason why *Full Fathom Five* is unburdened by any lengthy text—the Museum of Modern Art is one of the busiest museums in the world, and it must keep "traffic" flowing). If there were a label, however, it might read something like this:

> POLLOCK, Jackson. *Full Fathom Five.* 1947. Oil on canvas, with nails, tacks, buttons, key, coins, cigarettes, matches, etc. 50⅞ x 30⅛ in. Gift of Peggy Guggenheim.

> This painting is one of the first canvases in which Pollock intro-
> duced the "allover" method for which he is famous. By dripping
> or pouring his paint from sticks or hardened brushes onto canvas
> tacked to the floor, he was able to liberate his paintings from any
> sense of being subjected to the inhibiting constraints of tradi-
> tional, conscious technique. They seemed to spring, now, from
> unconscious sources. Pollock's title, then, taken from Ariel's song
> in Act I of Shakespeare's *The Tempest*, suggests a movement below
> the surface of things and into the unconscious, into a world where
> painting is transformed, in Ariel's words, into "something rich
> and strange."

I have limited myself here to approximately 100 words, pretty
much the maximum that the public can readily assimilate from a
label accompanying an individual work of art. I could, of course,
say a great deal more—but the very fact that much more can be
said is precisely why, as a writer, you can gain not only a great
deal of information from labels such as this, but valuable direction for further research and inquiry as well. When you read
(and copy down) the information on a label, almost inevitably
you will recognize what other information might be of value to
you. Given the label above, you would of course look up the
reference to Shakespeare in order to see if there is, in Ariel's
song, anything else that might be of use—and there is, as I have
already suggested. You would almost certainly want to look at
the paintings Pollock executed in 1946 just before this work—
some samples of which are in fact close by in the Museum of
Modern Art—in order to look at how the "inhibiting constraints
of traditional, conscious technique" are evident in these earlier
paintings. You might want to know about Pollock's interest in
the unconscious, and this information, in turn, would probably
lead you both to Pollock's own experiences in psychoanalysis and
to the influence on Pollock of the French Surrealists, many of
whom arrived in New York in the early 1940s in order to escape
the war in Europe: they emphasized in their own art a kind of
composition based on "psychic automatism," the dictation of
thought in the absence of all control by reason. You might discover, at this point, that many of these French artists circulated
around Peggy Guggenheim, who was married to one of them,
and that Pollock exhibited almost exclusively at Peggy Guggenheim's gallery—suddenly the brief citation on the label, "Gift
of Peggy Guggenheim," takes on a greater resonance. You
might want to read the criticism in order to get a better idea of

precisely what that word "allover" implies. You might even want to follow the history of Pollock's pouring technique as it developed in subsequent years—especially as it relates to the world of images—or his use of concrete things (combs, nails, and so on), which reemerge in his painting after 1950 but which, in *Full Fathom Five*, seem at the brink of completely disappearing beneath the swirl of his paint. There seems to be, in other words, an interesting tension, or dialectic, in Pollock's painting between what he calls "pure painting," on the one hand, and reference to the real world, on the other. The relation between the two might be worth exploring. Again, in the Museum of Modern Art there are examples not only of paintings from 1947 to 1950 in which all reference to the world at large seems to have disappeared, but also of later paintings in which recognizable images, even a portrait, reassert themselves.

This is all to suggest that a very substantial essay might easily be developed out of a careful examination of a painting like *Full Fathom Five* and that the conception of this essay would be greatly facilitated by paying attention to the relatively few words which surround the painting as a verbal frame. They are meant to help and inform you. Take advantage of them.

CONSULTING ARTISTS' STATEMENTS AND EXHIBITION CATALOGUES

Very often, especially in one-person exhibitions, an artist's statement, sometimes accompanied by a *curriculum vita* or brief history of previous exhibitions and writings about the artist's work, will be available, either in leaflet form or prominently displayed as a part of the exhibition. The quality of artists' statements varies widely; one sometimes feels that, asked by a curator or gallery director to provide something of the kind, and feeling, as Pollock did, that the work should stand on its own, or that language betrays it, or perhaps out of sheer lack of verbal skill, the artist misrepresents what is going on in the art, intentionally or otherwise. In other words, artists' statements must be approached with caution. However, if they seem to help your analysis of the work, then by all means consider them.

A short statement by Pollock will serve as an example. These comments did not actually accompany an exhibition but were published in a small magazine called *Possibilities* in 1947.

Pollock almost certainly considered them to be an "explanation" of what he was up to in his painting, and almost every critic who has come to grips with his art since has relied on them, perhaps because there is so little else to rely on. They have, at any rate, become so central to our understanding of his work that if a one-person retrospective of Pollock's painting were to be mounted today, the statement would almost surely be printed prominently in the exhibition space itself:

> When I am *in* my painting, I'm not aware of what I'm doing. It is only after a sort of "get acquainted" period that I see what I have been about. I have no fears about making changes, destroying the image, etc., because the painting has a life of its own. I try to let it come through. It is only when I lose contact with the painting that the result is a mess. Otherwise there is pure harmony, an easy give and take, and the painting comes out well.[2]

The famous first sentence—"When I am *in* my painting, I'm not aware of what I'm doing"—refers of course to Pollock's insistence on his painting's attachment to the unconscious. The most useful phrase here, however, occurs at the end. What Pollock does in this statement is provide you with a vocabulary which you can use to describe his painting—"pure harmony" and "easy give and take." These are things he wants to achieve, and you need to examine the work itself in order to decide for youself in what ways an "easy give and take" or a "pure harmony" seems to be in evidence. You might argue, for instance, that the tension between the world of things and the world of "pure painting" is embodied in the "give and take" of line as it begins to delineate form or shape and then flies off free. Or you might say that, because Pollock's surface seems to be uniform in intensity, he achieves a sense of "pure harmony." In other words, this vocabulary gives you a way in, something to look for. It helps you to articulate what you see.

The catalogues that sometimes accompany exhibitions can be of even greater help. Even if all the catalogue provides you with is reproductions of the works that interest you most, it can be an invaluable aid in writing your essay, a ready reference once you go home. Be sure, however, that the color in the reproductions is accurate: compare them with the works themselves (don't trust your memory of the color), and if the reproductions are in black and white, note the actual colors separately. Often the catalogue will contain essays to help you understand the exhibition in general as well as individual works. When you are writing about works of art that are accompanied by such a catalogue, it is best to read the essays *after* your first visit and *after* you have begun to form opinions of your own. Even though the essays are usually written by leading experts, you need not necessarily consider them the absolute last word on the works. The best writing about art—and this is as true of professional writing as it is of student writing—raises as many questions as it answers. You should approach catalogue essays in the spirit of initiating a dialogue with them. Let them suggest things to you, let them initiate a line of thought for you to follow that you might not have pursued without their lead, but do not let them have the final word. *Use* the essays, certainly, but to support your *own* thinking.

DISCOVERING OTHER HELPFUL MATERIAL IN THE LIBRARY

One of the most useful things about exhibition catalogues is that they contain bibliographies of what has been written about a given artist's work. (The *curriculum vita* of the artist at a one-person show will often contain a bibliography as well.) If you are writing a major research paper on a relatively well-known artist, the best way to begin is to consult the most recent catalogue you can find and to compile as current a bibliography as possible on the particular aspect of the work that interests you.

The preceding sentence contains two notions about the best ways to begin writing about art that have been implicit assumptions of this text from the outset. First, it is important, especially as you begin writing about art, to begin in the particular. It is far easier to write a paper on *Full Fathom Five* than it is on Jackson Pollock—let alone some even larger topic like "American Abstract Painting 1940 to the Present." A well-reasoned essay on the particular painting would inevitably lead you to some interesting conclusions about Pollock and on American abstract painting as well.

Second, I have assumed that you do not always have to write a major "research" paper, that much of your writing about art, from essays on examinations to more formal assignments, will depend more on simply your ability to ask the right questions about works of art. Inevitably, these simpler writings should lead you to a situation where a larger, more ambitious paper might be not merely possible but something you actually want to do. Still, it may not be necessary to consult secondary sources in the library in order to write a good paper about contemporary or relatively unknown work. Obviously, if the work refers directly to something you don't know—Shakespeare, say, or a Greek myth—then you will have to do a little independent research. But many intelligent papers have been written about art without their authors consulting any sources outside the immediate context of the work itself—its title and label, an accompanying artist's statement, and so on. On the other hand, when you are writing about a relatively well-known work of art or artist, your approach might well benefit from a consideration of the opinions of the larger, well-informed community of scholars and critics. At its best, scholarship in art history can help you to understand the work more fully than you might have without it. At the very least, it should help you to frame the questions with which you will engage the work on your own.

If a major research effort is the order of the day, there are some ways to proceed that will save you time and result in a better paper. If you have the opportunity to write about works of art you can see in person, by all means do so. If you are working from "the museum without walls"—much more likely if you are writing a research paper—if at all possible choose to write about one or two particular works. If you must write about some larger topic—if, for instance, you have been asked to write about "a major issue in a nineteenth-century painting of your choice"—then approach the problem *through* one or two particular paintings. In other words, find works that seem to embody in some way the problem at hand, and draw your larger conclusions from a detailed examination of them. There are many advantages to working this way, some of which will be discussed later, but it should be clear that your conclusions will be far more defensible—and seem more sensible—to a reader who has watched you fashion them out of your detailed analysis of particular works.

Using the Card Catalogue and Scanning Books

Begin your research by locating discussions of the one or two works you have chosen to consider in detail. If you were writing on Pollock's *Full Fathom Five*, for instance, it would take very little time for you to check the various books on Pollock in your library for references to the painting. Go first to the card catalogue. Every book in your library is included, filed not only by author and title, but also by subject. Try to avoid the headings included under "Art." "Art: American—20th Century" occupies over two and a half drawers in my library, and thumbing through them all, looking for the references to Pollock, can be a numbing experience. Instead look up "Pollock, Jackson." There you can quickly find all the books about him. If you have trouble locating material, that may be because you have focused your subject too narrowly; for instance, *"Full Fathom Five"* would not have a separate subject heading in the card catalogue. If you continue to have difficulty, ask the reference librarian, who will help you locate the subject area heading where you have the best chance of discovering appropriate material. A word of warning: the more contemporary your subject matter, the less likely it is that you will find reference to it in the card catalogue. You will have to work from magazines and journals.

I am assuming, of course, that you know which particular works you want to write about. You should have some idea of what interests you from your experience in class, but if you don't, or if you prefer to discuss works that have not been dealt with in class, then go to the library and look up the general area that you have been asked to consider; for example, if your assignment is to consider any "major issue in nineteenth-century painting of your choice," look up "Art: 19th Century—France." Or you may know you want to write about Corot's landscapes, but you aren't sure which ones. Look up "Corot" (and possibly "Landscape—19th Century"). You will notice that most of the books on a particular subject have the same general call number; this is so because many of the books in the art section of the library are grouped in the stacks first by medium, then, as sub-groups, by nationality, and, finally, within each country of origin, alphabetically by artist. (If you write very many papers, you will soon get to know which shelves contain what books. You will know where French or American painting is, where the sculpture books are, and so on.) Go to the area of the stacks that contains works on your general topic, find books with a lot of good reproductions in them, then sit down and look through them until you discover something that interests you and that seems rich enough to generate a good essay.

Once you have compiled the basic books on your subject,

check their indexes for reference to the particular works you want to discuss. If the discussions seem useful or significant, then read them in more detail. Also look at the footnotes to the passages that discuss the works. These might lead you to other important discussions. If a book contains no specific reference to the works in question (some books are badly indexed or indexed not at all), scan tables of contents: does the book sound interesting anyway? Consider who published the books—a major art book publisher, a university press, a major museum? All of these are some indication of quality. Finally consider how recently the book has been published. The most recent publications, expecially catalogues and university press publications, will often incorporate and build upon previous scholarship. You can often avoid plowing through much earlier material by reading discussions of it in later publications. If the earlier work seems interesting and important, by all means return to it, but sometimes it will seem, in the light of more recent scholarship, antiquated or irrelevant.

Consulting Indexes

At this point, after you have some general notion of how much material there is on the works of art you've chosen to concentrate on, and after you've gotten some sense of the parameters of the critical discussion surrounding them, consult the *Art Index*. This is a basic research tool with which all art students need to be acquainted. It is almost always housed in the reference area of your library. Ask the reference librarian. The *Art Index* is a year-by-year bibliography, organized alphabetically by subject matter, of the major art journals and magazines. If you were writing on a painting by Jackson Pollock, you would look up "Pollock, Jackson," and there you would find all the articles and essays written about him in the year of the volume you are looking at. Begin with the most recent year of coverage and work your way back. If there is a lot of writing on your particular subject, then five years ought to be sufficient. If there is very little, you may want to go back for ten years. Just as more recent books tend to incorporate and build upon older scholarship, so do more recent essays in the art journals and magazines. Any important older scholarship will almost certainly be mentioned in the more recent essays.

The *Art Index* offers another important feature. Besides listing each article and essay, and giving you some idea of the reproductions accompanying each, it lists by title reproductions of individual works by each artist: what is especially useful is that it also includes reproductions appearing in gallery advertisements and the like. If you are having trouble locating a color reproduction of a work that you've seen only in black and white, you can generally find a color reproduction—if one in fact exists—by patiently working your way through the *Art Index* year by year.

RILA (*Répertoire international de la littérature de l'art*) is another extemely useful index. It has the disadvantage of covering only post-Classical western art—the *Art Index* provides by far the widest coverage—but it does include books in addition to journals and magazines. Futhermore, it has brief abstracts or summaries of all of the listed material. These can be especially useful if any of the books you need to consult is checked out of the library. You may determine, after consulting *RILA*, that you can do without it—or you may want to recall it. Sometimes also the *Art Index* may give a reference to an essay in a journal that your library doesn't own or that, for whatever reason, is missing. *RILA* can help you determine how important that particular essay might be to your argument.

No index, of course, can ever be completely up-to-date. It generally takes at least a couple of years to put together a single volume. Thus, in 1988 you will perhaps be able to find 1985 or 1986 volumes, but nothing more recent. There is only one thing you can do. You will, at some point late in your research, have some idea of which journals and magazines show the most interest in your particular subject matter. If you go through the most recent issues of these publications, often you will discover an important recent piece of scholarship.

Using Art Dictionaries

Many times, when you write a more sophisticated paper involving research, you will run across technical vocabulary with which you are unfamiliar. This happens even to the most highly trained art historians and critics. By all means, take the time to look up things you don't know. Your paper will almost always benefit from the extra effort. The *Adeline Art Dictionary* is an extremely useful summary of specialized terms used in the various fine arts media. It will be housed at the reference desk of your library. If you find you need help with terms or concepts that do not appear in *Adeline*, ask your reference librarian.

CONSIDERING
THE HISTORICAL CONTEXT

The largest verbal frame surrounding a work of art—larger even than the body of critical and art historical discussions about it—has to do with its place in the larger scheme of things, art historical and otherwise. Each work is conceived in a particular time and in a particular place, and to some degree it is bound to reflect the circumstances of its conception. Cubism, for instance, developed in Paris between 1907 and 1912 as a group style which defined itself not only in relation to much of the painting that had preceded it—Cézanne's late paintings of *Mont Sainte-Victoire* were exhibited in 1907 after his death and were very influential—but also in the context of a rapidly developing and changing social milieu. Between 1890 and the outbreak of World War I in August, 1914 the pace of European life was dramatically accelerated, its continuities were disrupted, and its verities undermined. The internal combustion and diesel engines began to power the machines which transported people not only long distances but to their very jobs. Electricity replaced gas light in the streets, and these streets were no longer filled with horses and carriages but, suddenly, with automobiles. In 1900 there were 3,000 automobiles in all of France, but by 1907 that number had jumped to 30,000 and by 1913 France was itself *producing* 45,000 automobiles a year. Henry Adams, visiting the 1900 World's Fair in Paris, after looking out across the complex of electric dynamos which powered the fair, noted that "the planet itself seemed less impressive, in its old-fashioned, deliberate, annual or daily revolution, than this huge wheel, revolving within arm's-length at some vertiginous speed." He found himself, he said, "lying in the Gallery of Machines at the Great Exposition of 1900, with his historical neck broken by the sudden irruption of forces totally new."[3] Soon airplanes and zeppelins floated across the Parisian skies. In offices, which a generation earlier had been the realm of scriveners and copyists, the routine of day-to-day business was transformed by the telephone, the typewriter, and the tape recorder. The daily newspaper became an institution. Cinemas began to spring up everywhere. In 1905 Einstein published his Special Theory of Relativity, and soon Bohr offered a new model of the atom. As Robert Wohl put it in an essay on the generation of 1914: "Everything was in flux. Old systems of reference were under attack, old hierarchies were being challenged, and old elites were being pressed to make concessions. Revolution seemed inevitable and those who had something to lose did not conceal their fear."[4] As a style of art, Cubism seemed to embody this upheaval. It reflected, that is, the rapid change and, above all, the "revolutionary" drift of the twentieth century itself. If it was not received with universal enthusiasm, that is because, symbolically at least, it represented the end of one era and the dawn of a new, uncertain future.

The same sorts of context could be, and have been, developed for almost any recognizable period style. Courbet's realism can be usefully tied to the social upheavals in Europe in 1848, and David's Neoclassicism to the French Revolution in 1789. The naturalism that marks Giotto's painting in the early fourteenth century, especially noticeable when compared with the flat, almost abstract medieval formulas for representation that are typical of the painting that precedes him, can be said to inaugurate the Renaissance. Above all, Giotto creates *believable* people, who seem to possess highly personal feelings and a sense of their own individuality. This new "humanism," or an interest in the potential and capacity of each individual human being, can be seen throughout Renaissance art, literature, and philosophy.

Needless to say, the more you know about a given period, the more easily you will be able to place whatever works of art you are discussing from that period within a larger context. For this reason, my university requires art history students to take a sequence of courses on the history of western civilization either before or concurrently with their art history courses, and I often advise students registering for, say, Nineteenth-Century French Painting to take a course concurrently in nineteenth-century French history or literature.

In the end, however, you will do far better to define, in your paper, the particular qualities that contribute to the power and interest of *Full Fathom Five,* for instance, than to try to fit *Full Fathom Five* into some preconceived notion of American Abstract Expressionism or the history of post-World War II American culture. There are, for one thing, widely varying ideas about what, precisely, Abstract Expressionism even is, let alone how it came to be the most important art movement in the world in the 1950s. One school of thought sees it as a kind of painting which is interested in painting for its own sake—"pure paint-ing," as Pollock himself put it. For them, his greatest paintings are the great numbered works of 1947–1950 which have no overt reference. A second group sees Abstract Expressionism as the record of an event—the painting becomes the record, as it were, of Pollock's physical and mental activity. Still others are interested in the way the idea of representation seems to be contested in the paintings, and this group is especially interested in Pollock's inclusion of more representational elements in his painting after 1950 and in the way that his more abstract works tend to bury representational elements under layers of paint, as if he is repressing them. This final insight, futhermore, offers those who would like to read Pollock's painting in psychoanalytic terms a way to deal with it from yet another perspective.[5] Well, which is the best approach to *Full Fathom Five?* Even if you have an opinion—and if you're like me, you're tempted to like some-thing in all of them—you should see that "fitting" your discus-sion into any one of these schemes is likely to cause you more problems than not.

In the end, the best advice I can give you is that when you feel comfortable with the various jargons of period and group styles, use them. But use them cautiously, and try to avoid approaching individual works of art with the preconceptions they tend to engender. Most Picassos, after all, are far richer than the word "cubist" will ever indicate.

QUOTING AND DOCUMENTING YOUR SOURCES

Learning the Art of Quoting

The greatest danger that students confront when they write research papers is that their final paper will contain, in the end, nothing of their own but will be a sort of compendium of appropriate quotations. This is equally true, incidentally, of doc-toral students and freshmen. Many a doctoral thesis is overbur-dened by references. It is a failing that is easy to understand: why speak for yourself when so many more informed people can speak for you? And besides, you want the professor to see how much research you've done. Remember, however, that it is *your* mind that the professor wants to see at work, not that of some famous critic.

Here is a rule of thumb for fitting quotations into your writing: *When you quote, always move on from the quotation and continue the paragraph by developing the idea the quotation initiates.* Earlier in this chapter it was suggested that you approach critical essays in the spirit of initiating a dialogue with them. By forcing yourself to respond, as it were, to the material you quote, you will in fact begin just such a dialogue. You will never become a slave to your research. Also, in a very real sense, by responding to it and developing it further, you will make the quoted material your own. It becomes part of your argument, not something outside your argument to which you have deferred.

In other words, there is a real art to quoting. You want to quote things that are especially informative or well written. Such material tends to elevate the quality of your own prose. As in playing tennis, you tend to play to the level of your opposition; this is not to say, however, that you should quote only opinions with which you can argue. Some of the best passages in papers are those in which something is said well in a quotation and then the student, in the particular context of the argument at hand, says it better. Perhaps you have noticed that in this book other critics have been quoted in precisely this way. Joshua Taylor's discussion of the Perugino and Crivelli crucifixions is a classic piece of art historical writing. I tried to elevate my own discussion by incorporating Taylor's argument into my own, but I built on Taylor's distinctions, and I used them to my own ends. The discussion of Perugino and Crivelli in Chapter 2 was developed, in fact, to provide you with a model for quoting authoritative sources. Refer to it when you want to quote secondary sources (and be sure to note that the quotation furthers an argument that continues after the quotation itself). Good writing tends to stimulate more good writing. When you read criticism, look not only for useful information but also for the well-turned phrase, the interesting and informative anecdote, the particularly insightful analysis of a work of art. These things can do more than inform you, they can provide a foundation upon which to build your own essay.

Acknowledging Your Sources

I am constantly surprised at the number of students who seem to be embarrassed that they have consulted research materials. To the contrary, doing so shows energy, interest, and determination. The only times you need to worry about using such materials—except of course when the professor, for whatever reason, asks you not to consult secondary sources—is when you have done a superficial job, consulting only one or two books or articles and, more important, when you have not acknowledged that you have done so. If you do research, do it well. If you appropriate phrases, whole passages, ideas—even if you've put these in your own words—or the logic of an argument from someone else, and you fail to acknowledge it, then you have plagiarized the work. The penalties for plagiarism vary from school to school, but they are never very pleasant.

The point is that if you use research materials well—as the beginning of your own argument, not as an end in themselves— then you need never be embarrassed to cite these materials. In fact, one of the checks you can use to judge the quality of your own paper is to determine at the draft stage just how much of *you* there is in the paper. If you detect more of your absence from the argument than your presence, if you feel that one solution might be to go back and convert some quotations "into your own words," then you have probably not entered into a dialogue with the criticism so much as let the criticism rule you. In order to revise, engage the criticism, see if you can push its ideas further, perhaps by using it to analyze a particular work.

You do not, of course, need to footnote or acknowledge anything that could be considered common knowledge—dates of birth and death, the location of paintings, historical facts, the definitions of widely used words, and so on. Generally, if a question of interpretation seems to enter into the material, or if the fact seems genuinely new, then by all means cite your source. When in doubt, play it safe. But again, watch for overcitation. If you consistently have more than two or three footnotes per typed page, then something is wrong—either you are acknowledging things you need not acknowledge or your argument is too dependent on outside sources.

Choosing Your Footnote Style

Footnote conventions in art history differ widely. They depend, among other things, on where the article or book you are reading was published. The British have one system; the Americans another. Even in the United States, conventions differ from publication to publication: *Art in America* has its own ideas about what a footnote should look like, while *The Art Bulletin* has a completely different set of standards. The footnotes that have been used in this book should give you an idea of the style suggested by *The Chicago Manual of Style*, a style preferred by many book publishers. In all styles, however, a few general rules apply. Generally, in order to designate a footnote, simply put a raised number after the final punctuation of the sentence, unless there are several references in a single sentence (something you should work to avoid). Number the notes consecutively and put them at the end of the paper. (There is simply no advantage to putting notes at the bottom of the page. The typing can prove to be extraordinarily difficult, and the professor can easily remove the note pages from the back of the paper and keep them beside the text while reading anyway. However, if you put your footnotes at the end of the paper, do *not* staple the pages together. Put the paper in a loose-leaf folder or use a high-quality paper clip.) Double-space your notes just as you would your paper, to facilitate legibility. If you are using a computer your software may not elevate numbers. In this case, it is probably acceptable to put each note in parentheses at the end of the appropriate sentence.

Each footnote itself is, in effect, a sentence. Type the number—either raised or followed by a period—and then type the footnote as if it were a sentence in its own right. It will begin with a capital letter and end with a period. Conventions do vary greatly, however. Outlined below are two alternative styles for your consideration.

The Chicago Style. In the Chicago Style each footnote is a sort of mini-paragraph, and so it is indented. Briefly, for a *book*, the Chicago Style form is the following:

1. Author(s), <u>Title</u> (Place of Publication: Publisher, Date of Publication), page number(s).

The author's name appears in its normal sequence—given name, initial(s), and surname—followed by a comma. The title is underlined. There is no punctuation between the title and the parentheses, but there is a comma after the parenthetical information (all of which can usually be found on the back of the title page), and then the page numbers are listed, without the abbreviations "p." or "pp." The note ends with a period. If there is an editor or translator to the edition you are using, follow the title with a comma and place that information before the parenthetical information, again followed by no punctuation. Examples of all these forms can be found in the Notes section at the end of this text.

In order to refer to an article or essay in a *journal* or *magazine*, use this form:

2. Author(s), "Title of Article," Name of Journal Vol # (Date of Publication): page number(s).

In this case the title of the article is in quotation marks and the name of the journal underlined. There is no punctuation either between the journal name and the volume number or between the volume number and the date of publication. The date of publication is put in parentheses and is followed by a colon. The page numbers, again, are not introduced by "p." or "pp." If there are no page numbers, as there often are not in art publications, simply put "unpaginated." Again, there are examples in the Notes section at the end of this text.

When you make *subsequent references* to a work you've already cited in full, you may shorten your note. I still prefer "Ibid." to refer to exactly the same material as in the immediately preceding note (this is an abbreviation for the Latin *ibidem*, meaning "in the same place"). Some people, however, simply prefer to use a shortened note. For instance, you would refer to a work already cited by just the author's last name and the appropriate page number, or, if you have referred to more than one work by the same author, the last name plus a shortened version of the title and then the page number. Always use such a shortened form for subsequent references that refer to works cited earlier than the previous note. Again, examples of all these forms are included in the notes to this book. If you do a lot of writing, you might want to purchase the *Chicago Manual*, but the reference desk in almost every library will have a copy of it. For difficult footnote problems, consult it. Almost every imaginable contingency is anticipated.

The Art Bulletin Style. A second possible footnote style is that of *The Art Bulletin*, among the most prestigious of the art history journals. It differs considerably from the Chicago Style. *The Art Bulletin* employs what is known as the "short form" method of citation. Footnotes are *not* indented, as in the Chicago Style, though they are doubled-spaced. You elevate the footnote number, skip a space, and then type the note. The note consists of the author's surname and the page number (e.g., [1] Smith, 243), separated by a comma. If there are two or more publications by "Smith" cited in your text, they are distinguished by date of publication ([1] Smith, 1943, 243). Books by the same author that have the same date of publication should be designated "a," "b," "c," and so on ([1] Smith, 1943a, 243). As in the Chicago Style, Ibid. replaces "Smith" if the reference is to the work cited in the immediately preceding note.

The "short form" may seem far less cumbersome at first glance, but it requires a full bibliography at the end of the essay. The citations are listed in alphabetical order by author. Here are representative examples of the bibliographic form for both books and articles drawn from the March 1985 number of *The Art Bulletin* (which also contains, on its last page, a somewhat fuller account of its footnote style than that outlined here):

Drexler, A., ed., *The Architecture of the Ecole des Beaux-Arts*, Cambridge, Mass., 1974.

Gimpel, J., *The Cathedral Builders*, New York, 1983.

Saalman, H., "Early Renaissance Architectural Theory and Practice in Antonio Filarete's Trattato di Architettura," *Art Bulletin*, XLI, 1959, 89–106.

Smith, W., *Medieval Painting*, 2nd ed., Paris, 1925.

Strauss, W. L., *The Complete Drawings of Albrecht Dürer*, 6 vols., New York, 1974.

White, J., 1973, "Measurement, Design and Carpentry in Duccio's Maestà," *Art Bulletin*, LV, Pt. I, 334–66; Pt. II, 547–69.

———, 1979, *Duccio: Tuscan Art and the Medieval Workshop*, London.

Notice, in these last two examples, that the second listing is indicated with an extended underline (five spaces) and that the date has been moved forward after the author's name to help distinguish more quickly between works by the same author. Notice also that a journal's volume is indicated in Roman rather than Arabic numbers and that no publishers are listed.

It is useful to keep in mind that footnote styles are not meant to confuse you, though they almost inevitably seem diabolically complicated to most beginning writers. They are meant to be straightforward references for your reader's information and convenience. There is, in the end, a very easy set of principles which can guide you in developing your notes: be as brief as your sense of full citation will allow, be logical, be consistent, and be clear. If you err, err in the direction of providing too much information. If you feel confusion set in, get help from the *Chicago Manual* or consult a recent issue of *The Art Bulletin*.

4

WORKING WITH WORDS AND IMAGES
The Process of Writing About What You See

GATHERING TOGETHER WHAT YOU KNOW

There are many places to begin the process of writing about a particular work of art. Once you've chosen what you're going to discuss, once you've looked at it carefully for a while, the point comes when you must put pen to paper—or, as is often the case these days, create a filename for your software—and begin. Many people never fully discover what it is they think until they begin to write. The process of writing in itself can free you to articulate what you think. Being forced to write something down sometimes helps you to make up your mind.

The process of writing should begin as early as possible—from the first moments you enter a gallery if that is at all practicable. Jot down your feelings, your initial impressions, which painting or sculpture attracts you first. You might even want to note which items seem totally uninteresting. Then give yourself a chance, later, to see if these apparently "uninteresting" works are still with you. If they are, there might be more to them than you originally thought, something worth investigating and developing. Above all, don't suppose that you will remember how you felt, that you will be able to recreate the process of choices and decisions that finally leads you to your interest in a particular work. When I review exhibitions or shows, I first quickly tour the gallery or exhibition space, taking notes, diagraming the rooms, noting what intrigues me, what alienates me, and what seems less than important. Depending on the show, I might jot down titles, dates, the names of painters. If I quickly recognize a direction of thought I want to pursue, I'll make notes about that. If there seem to be any exceptional highlights, works around which I sense I could focus a discussion, I'll note those down as well.

Then I leave. I go out to the lobby, or to a restaurant, or to a nearby park bench, and reread my notes. In a short time I have a pretty good sense of what I need to go back to see. I make notes about possible lines of thought to pursue, questions that seem to be raised, works I need to look at more intently. I generally try to ask myself a couple of questions that will force me to consider works I might otherwise ignore. I might even jot down in my notebook—and I have done it—how could anybody (i.e., the curator or the painter or whomever) interested in "x" (which I like) also be interested in "y" (which I don't)? I'll look at all those things I don't like in order to see what, if any, redeeming qualities I can discover in them.

This process doesn't take a very long time. I usually like to make a quick short visit before lunch, followed by a more leisurely and more intense viewing afterwards. I almost always have a good sense of what I want to say, and which works I want to concentrate my discussion around, within a half hour of my return visit. Then the real work of writing begins.

FOCUSING YOUR DISCUSSION

If you read many discussions about art, you will quickly notice that the most readable and interesting of them almost always focus on particular works. If you go back and look at whatever section of this book has seemed to you the most interesting, you will probably find that it is a particular discussion of a particular work. In other words, I could discuss something like color theory all day at a fairly abstract level, but what makes it interesting, in the end, is Van Gogh's particular application of color in *The Night Café*. Similarly, as a writing tactic, for the discussion in the last chapter I tried to find an interesting example of a work whose title and medium both mattered, Pollock's *Full Fathom*

Five, in order to sustain your interest (and in order, of course, to be convincing). Consider how dry the previous chapters might have been without particular examples and sometimes highly detailed analysis. Then consider how likely you would have been to get much out of them without those examples.

In other words, this art textbook, like many others, is organized by the principle of using extended discussions of particular works to make more general points. When art appreciation or art history professors analyze works of art in class, they are usually providing you with the same sorts of models. Ground your own writings in the concrete discussion of particular works. Focus on the specific problems of form, design, and content that they raise. You will almost always discover that in the process of describing and analyzing particular works, you will arrive at more general conclusions that you did not anticipate.

What are the advantages of writing in this way? In the first place, when you begin to write, you do not know precisely where you are going, what your conclusions will be. This approach to writing does run somewhat counter to the rationale of outline making. Outlines have their function—they provide a way for you to organize your ideas and present them in an orderly way—but if you let order supplant inspiration so that you find yourself filling out the skeleton of your outline to the necessary 1,000 or 2,000 words, then both the process of writing your essay and the essay itself will be boring. Often I can look at a group of student essays and tell who worked from outlines from the outset and who didn't. The giveaway is that in an essay first conceived in outline form, the introduction and the conclusion are almost always virtually the same. A skilled writer will manage to alter the language a little, but the substance will not change. This occurs because, as the writer begins, the essay's conclusions are already predetermined. In contrast, an essay that begins as a process of discovery and exploration almost always ends differently than it begins. It discovers something it didn't anticipate. It articulates connections it could at first only intuit. The second kind of essay is almost always more interesting to read. It seems to be engaged. It seems active, whereas the other kind of essay, no matter how "right" it might be, seems static in comparison.

In order to outline effectively and avoid being trapped in a predetermined set of assumptions, it can be useful to think of your main and subordinate ideas in terms of the questions they raise. If you were to write about Pollock's *Full Fathom Five*, you might begin your outline like this:

I. The significance of the title
   A. Reference to Shakespeare
      1. Idea of death
      2. Idea of transformation (i.e., "sea-change")
   B. Relation to technique
      1. Allover effect of canvas (i.e., abstraction)
      2. Submergence of recognizable objects in paint
II. The idea of surface and depth

Behind this outline, however, lies a series of questions. How do death and transformation go together? What kind of "death" is evident in the canvas? Does it display the death of "representation," of the "object"? What has "representation" been "transformed" into? If Pollock has transformed representation (or reference to the world of things) into abstraction, is abstraction a matter of "surface"? If so, does representation still lie hidden in the painting's depths? These questions, of course, are not easy to answer, and though you might have some idea of the direction in which you need to go after having arrived at the outline, the territory remains uncharted and interesting to explore.

Whether or not you choose to outline beforehand, the completed essay should be susceptible to outlining. That is, it should develop in a logically controlled and chartable way. For those writers who find outlining an overly restrictive way to begin writing—and there are many—there are other ways to begin. Depending on your temperament, any of the methods described in the next sections, or some combination of them, perhaps even including outlining, might suit you.

Brainstorming

I began to organize this book by brainstorming. In other words, I made a random list of topics and subjects that I thought

I should address in a book on writing about art. This is how the list began:

formal elements	indexes
principles of design	footnote form
the museum	the verbal frame
the museum without walls	words and images
the "white cube"	Arakawa's lemons
Duchamp's urinal	student essays
Joshua Taylor	outlining, prewriting, etc.
titles	revising

For several days I added to this list, and as I did so, certain patterns began to emerge. Some of these patterns were evident from the outset; for instance, a cluster of ideas about museums seemed important right away. Soon the titles of the four chapter headings presented themselves. I began to fill out the list in greater detail, grouping elements as I went. For instance, the phrase "the verbal frame" suggested a group of ideas for more particular development:

the "verbal frame" {
    Pollock's *Full Fathom Five*
    importance of title
    importance of medium

A whole page began to take shape under the heading "formal elements." I listed each formal element separately and jotted down ideas about how I might approach it:

Line
    — Taylor on crucifixions
        — use later to talk about quotation (?)
    — leads to discussion of space/perspective
        — Monet's *Gare St. Lazare*

Many ideas that occurred to me were eventually discarded. A great many notations, followed by question marks, served to indicate where I might tie discussions together. Some of these I followed up, some I never did. New ideas and modifications continued to occur throughout the writing process. Nevertheless, the essential drift of this book was in place in a matter of a few weeks.

Most of you will not be faced with taking on a project as large as this one, but you will find that the approach described is useful even if you have to write only a short paper. Furthermore, if you find outlining useful, brainstorming is a very good tool for generating your outline. It should be obvious that the material on "Line" above is really an informal outline, the beginnings of the much more formal shape the section on "Line" in this book would eventually take.

Using a Formal Description to Begin Writing

Another approach that is useful in writing about art is the formal description. There are two elements to a formal description: (1) a more or less straightforward description of the recognizable subject matter of the work, and (2) a summary of the various formal elements and principles of design at work in it. When you describe the subject matter of the work, by all means begin by mentioning the *title* and, if the title seems to contribute to your understanding of the subject matter, you will want to suggest what questions the title raises about the work. Like titles of novels or plays, titles of works of art are always italicized (underlined on the typewriter), since they are considered major works. You want, at any rate, to draw attention to the title because it is generally important. For instance, you can refer either to Marcel Duchamp's urinal, or to Duchamp's urinal entitled *Fountain* (Fig. 4). The second reference is far more suggestive and will lead, out of the simple accuracy and precision of your description, to a richer understanding of the work. What does it *mean* to call a urinal *Fountain*? You don't have to answer the question at this point, but it is important to raise it right away.

Begin your analysis of the formal elements of the work and how they are designed by noting the *medium* or *media* in which the work is executed. You would almost certainly see more significance in Pollock's *Full Fathom Five* were you to note its materials from the outset. And while it might take you a little time to discover the fact, it is important to know that E. Fay Jones's *Thorncrown Chapel* (Fig. 13) is made of gray-stained wood, not steel, in order for it to blend more effectively into the environment as a part of its natural surroundings.

Here is a formal description of Frederic Edwin Church's

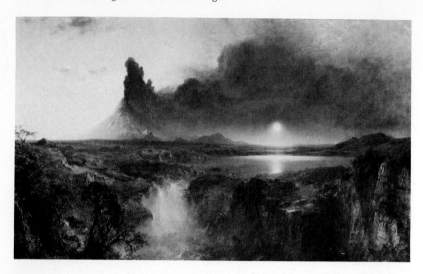

Figure 24   Frederic Edwin Church, *Cotopaxi*, 1862. Oil on canvas, 48 inches by 7 feet 1 inch. © 1987 The Detroit Institute of Arts, Founders Society purchase with funds from Mr. and Mrs. Richard A. Manoogian, Robert H. Tannahil Foundation Fund, Gibbs-Williams Fund, Dexter M. Ferry, Jr. Fund, Merrill Fund, and Beatrice W. Rogers Fund. Courtesy of the Detroit Institute of Arts.

Cotopaxi, Ecuador painted in 1862 (Fig. 24), written by an undergraduate student in a survey of nineteenth-century art course:

Frederic Edwin Church's <u>Cotopaxi, Ecuador</u> is a large, 48″ × 85″ oil painting of a volcano in eruption in South America. The horizon line cuts the canvas across the center, creating a sense of compositional balance to the scene. In the foreground are cliffs and jagged rocks, a chasm above which the viewer, more or less precariously, stands. This deep ravine, through which a river covered with mist must flow, leads back to a lake in the right center of the painting. Directly above the lake the sun is setting (or is it rising?). To the left, on the horizon, is Cotopaxi itself, spewing a plume of smoke upward to fill the entire right-hand corner of the canvas. Despite their difference in feel, the fiery volcano on the left is balanced by the bright light reflected in the lake on the right,

and that pattern of light forms a cross. The
curve of the clouds is repeated in the curve of
the water's edge by the rocks, making the sun
look, alternately, like the pupil of an ogre's
eyeball and the eye of God.

The scene seems simultaneously dangerous and
peaceful. Your eye is led up the river, around
the lake, through the smoke and always back to a
sort of double focus, the bright yellow sun and
the volcano, heaven and hell. On the one hand,
the sun reflects the stillness of the lake. On
the other, it seems closer to the molten energy
of the volcano. The smoke, jagged rocks, and
molten lava color of the scene all make you think
of the creation of the world. But then again, we
may be witnessing the end of the earth,
apocalypse. Everywhere there is strong contrast
between light and dark. It is as if the forces of
light were fighting with the forces of darkness.

In the lower left-hand corner a woman and what
looks like a donkey walk through the scene. They
are enveloped in the awesomeness of their
surroundings. The woman and donkey are so small
that it almost seems as if the artist were
implying that man is small and insignificant
compared to nature itself. The painting is large
enough that it reinforces this feeling.

This student has by no means exhausted the formal interest of Church's *Cotopaxi*, but there is evidence of a very
thoughtful analysis of the painting, and there is surely a lot of
good material here out of which to develop a much more substantial essay. Clearly, the most important issue that this writer
has located is the apparent tension in the painting between light
and dark, violence and calm, order and chaos, even heaven and
hell, and man's relative insignificance before such large and
unpredictable forces in the universe. As insightful as this is, it
amounts, nevertheless, to a kind of early draft in which the
writer is attempting to explore, through description, what possibilities the painting might hold for further discussion.

Most student papers never get past this stage. They
describe the work more or less adequately—or even very well—
but nothing more. You must go on, at this point, to ask what it all

means. Why has Church created this tension? Or, alternately, why does he insist on balancing opposite forces? Does he merely want to show us our insignificance before Nature, and if so, why? Why the careful division of the canvas into virtually symmetrical units? Is the sun in fact setting, or is it rising? (This is not so slight a question as it might at first appear—the answer dramatically affects the mood of the painting.) These are just a few of the questions that can be raised at this point, and that a good paper will continue to at least begin to answer.

This writer, in fact, did go on to do a great deal of research, and the resulting paper, which is far too long to reproduce here, considered *Cotopaxi* in relation to the writings of Ralph Waldo Emerson and Henry David Thoreau. Comparison was made, for instance, between Emerson's habit of contradicting himself as he sought a larger, more synthetic vision and the sense of "balanced opposition" one feels in the Church painting. Emerson's famous "transparent eyeball" passage, in which Emerson becomes, as he says, "part or parcel of God," becomes complicated, in Church's painting, by a more all-encompassing, larger, and finally less optimistic vision. Like Thoreau on Mt. Ktaadn in Maine, lost in the tortuous jumble of rocks and cliffs, Church recognizes that Nature is not always benign. Compositional balance, the author argued, was no longer employed so much to affect the sense of harmony and order both Emerson and Thoreau would have preferred as to create an almost modern "balance of power." In this light, *Cotopaxi* represents a revision of Emerson, a kind of "pragmatic transcendentalism."

Using Prewriting as a Way to Begin

Some students are more comfortable, at least initially, writing in a looser, somewhat more freewheeling style than the more systematic approach of the formal description. There are no rules in prewriting. Anything goes. The object, in fact, is to put down on paper as much as you can think of in a relatively limited amount of time. A lot of it you will probably later reject, but usually the basis for your essay can be developed out of this material.

The following is an example of the prewriting from which Amy Harrison, a student in a twentieth-century painting survey course, developed an essay on "Two Twentieth-Century Abstract Paintings." She wrote this at the computer in about forty minutes after looking at the two paintings in question, Vasily Kandinsky's *Tempered Elan* (Fig. 25) and Joan Miró's *Personnages rythmiques* (Fig. 26), for fifteen or twenty minutes. Notice that she isn't worried here about the niceties of punctuation, nor is she worried, at this point, about whether she's right or wrong. Her mind is simply wandering, as fast as it can, among the possibilities:

```
Miró uses blocks of color for a background uses
the curve a lot there are mirrored images like
the shape of the moon in the upper right hand
corner and the part of the body of the far left
figure the central figure seems to be a woman
looked at from different angles her breast shapes
are mirrored in the lower right hand figure. He
also uses solid dots and the moon is mirrored
again in the red and yellow shape there are also
repeating arches that cross other lines. The two
arches that are connected together give a sense
of perspective, depth. The smaller one that's
attached to the skinny figure puts that figure
behind the central one a couple of little faces
one of them looks mad the red and black shape on
the central figure's white body it looks at one
time like two separate things then another time
looks like the black is the underside of the red
and is twisted so we can see it. Lots of
contrasts between black, white, and red one shape
in the left background could be a tree with a
leaf on top get birth images amoebas or other
basic life forms. The central black arch that
cuts between the white and black part of the
central figure plays tricks on your eyes    you
see the white part as being separate from the
rest jumps away from the other part. The dot on
the central figure's breast seems to want to fall
off of it the line separating that breast and the
other half of the body creates an illusion that
the half bullseye is both separate and that the
black part blends in with the black breast. The
black and white alternating arches with the red
at the end also mirror the head that has
```

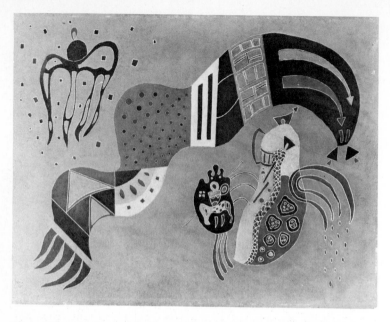

Figure 25   Vasily Kandinsky, *Tempered Elan*, 1944. Oil on cardboard,
16½ by 22⅞ inches. Collection: Musée National d'Art Moderne, Paris.

alternating red and black stripes with a white
one on one end. Miró seems to be playing with
perspective and illusions created by the eye.
Also the shapes seem to be floating about have
movement. They are rhythmic personnages a dance.
There are very few straight lines and where there
are they jump out seem misplaced everything
unstable growing changing rhythm of life. The
alternating color shapes and merely outlined
shapes give a sense of a game Inside the oval the
head of the central figure the red and the black
shapes each make a face, their lips meet in a
kiss

   Kandinsky--full of curved lines which are
contrasted with rectangle bars upper left hand
corner shape looks like a jellyfish symbolizing
primitive life the beginning the other shapes
also seem to be like primitive life forms. He
also plays with transparent space and colored
space especially the transparent jellyfish

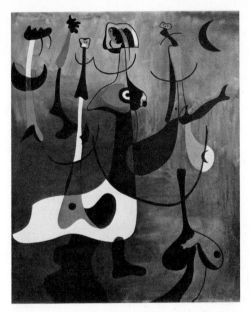

Figure 26 Joan Miró, *Personnages rythmi-*
ques, 1934. Oil on canvas 6 feet, 4 inches by 5
feet, 7⅜ inches. Kunstsammlung Nor-
drhein-Westfalen, Düsseldorf.

surround by solid square shapes played against
light shapes to create perspective the one bright
orange bar really jumps out at me looks separate
from the thing it's on. The red loop on the top
of the jellyfish is mirrored with the half red
triangle on top of the lower right hand figure
and the one inside the small dark figure has lots
of intricate design has same thing happening with
part of that figure as in Miró's painting the
rainbow on its right side looks like it's
continued out with the arches but the white line
also cuts them apart duality the arches also seem
to be taking away the life source of the shape.
Uses both geometric and organic shapes plays
colors against each other. The geometric forms
somewhat invade the organic shapes prevent them
from complete freedom the squares surround the
jellyfish, and the orange bar pins down the tail
of the large amoeba form the other smaller orange
bar pokes in the little dark form and comes out

the other side penetrating it. Lots of play with
design more intricate than the Miró everything
has a border to it and is completely filled or
completely empty no oozing like in the
Miró   less movement more static than
Miró   The clear space between the two dark
brown sections of the central figure really
stands out especially with its bright red
borders   He seems to want to keep life somehow
in the picture even when just playing with design
and color   The dark brown circle on top of the
jellyfish is like Miró's black dots   He
incorporates color, line, and object   A
movement toward an abstract design that's for
itself but at the same time leaves room for the
imagination to see something recognizable in the
painting   painting for the artist's sake but
not forgetting the viewer

Perhaps the most interesting thing that happens in this exercise is that, although the author begins by analyzing each painting separately, by the end of the section on Kandinsky she has begun to compare the two works. I think this is almost inevitable. What has happened is that after looking hard at the Miró she sees the Kandinsky in light of it. In some ways this approach distorts the Kandinsky—it wasn't painted, after all, to be seen in the context of the Miró—but it also helps the author recognize some of the special characteristics of both paintings. In particular "static" is not a word that one would normally think of when confronted by the Kandinsky, but next to the Miró it *is* comparatively static. This comparative stasis eventually led the author to make an important distinction between Miró's "fluid" abstraction and Kandinsky's "frozen" forms.

Comparative essays are the staple of art criticism and history because they tend to reveal just such interesting sorts of distinctions. Comparative procedures, in fact, could be said to be the very basis for arriving at *meaning*. If, for example, I say the word "tree," almost immediately an image springs to mind. And yet, the chances of the tree I'm thinking of corresponding to the tree you're thinking of are very slim indeed. Suppose I have been in southern France for the last few months and I have in mind the beautiful umbrella pines that can be seen all along the French Riviera. You, on the other hand, may be thinking of the tree in your backyard at home, or a Christmas tree, or a childlike drawing of a tree. The word itself—"tree"—while vaguely referring to a certain kind of plantlife, has very little real meaning until we begin to *particularize* it. We define each tree by employing language that distinguishes the particular tree we have in mind from the great mass of trees in general. We were all thinking of trees, but only in the act of comparing our thoughts do we begin to distinguish what each of us really means by the word.

Often, on examinations, you will be asked to compare and contrast various works, and the intention of the professor, believe it or not, is probably to help you see how two apparently different works might be alike in some special way, or how two similar works might be importantly different. Whatever the case, your discussion needs to be specific. If you begin a comparative essay on abstract painting, for instance, by saying, "These are both abstract paintings," you are effectively saying, "These are both trees." You are beginning, in other words, at a level of generalization from which you may or may not be able to rescue yourself. You are expecting understanding where there may be no real basis for it. However, if you begin your essay by formally describing one of the two works in question—probably the one with which you feel most comfortable—you will almost certainly approach the second in the light of what you've seen in the first. In this process you are likely to discover more than you initially thought you knew about the works in question. And you will communicate that discovery—that greater depth of learning—to your instructor.

CREATING A FINISHED ESSAY

Developing Your Thesis

A formal analysis of a work of art can be distinguished from its formal description by virtue of the fact that it takes into account the *meaning* of the formal elements it describes. It asks not only *what* artists have accomplished in formal terms, but *why* they have made the decisions they have. In other words, the function of the preliminary writing exercises suggested above is to help you discover ideas about the significance of the subject matter (the particular work or works of art) you have chosen to write about. They are designed to help you discover a *thesis*. For instance, Pollock's *Full Fathom Five* might be your subject matter, but your thesis consists of the central idea or point you wish to make about the painting. If you were to write a short paper on *Full Fathom Five*, you might state your thesis in terms such as this: *While, at first glance, Pollock's painting seems to be little more than a random web of lines representing nothing, it can be approached more productively as an investigation of the possibilities of representation itself.* Such a thesis statement marks the difference between the kind of writing samples presented so far and the next example, which was built out of the prewriting exercise that we have just examined. Early in this text I said that all art involves conscious decisions, and I suggested that one way for you to recognize these decisions is to imagine other possible handlings of the particular work you are examining. Good comparative essays offer the most appropriate format in which you can recognize this kind of difference, which is after all a difference in intention and meaning. The real point of Amy Harrison's final essay—her thesis—is that although Kandinsky and Miró have initiated their paintings from what appears to be similar positions, they have made formal decisions which make for very different effects and which seem in the end to have very different meanings. The final draft of her essay concludes as follows:

> Miró portrays organic, amoeba-like shapes which
> create a biomorphic design. His "personnages"
> seem to be alive. They seem to move in a rhythmic
> dance through the space of his canvas.
> Kandinsky's design is more intricate. Rather than
> creating a harmonious movement through space, his
> shapes--on the one hand, organic, and on the
> other, geometric--seem at odds with each other.
> The geometric shapes <u>invade</u> the organic shapes,
> as if to hold them back and keep them from
> attaining their freedom: squares surround
> jellyfish, the orange bar pins down the cilia of
> the large amoeba, the smaller orange bar
> penetrates the little dark form, the frame
> contains them all like a prison. Each shape seems
> complete, filled and outlined.
>   For Miró , abstraction is a fluid <u>process</u>. It
> is a kind of movement, a rhythm and flow through

space. For Kandinsky, this movement, this energy,
as his title indicates, is <u>tempered</u>. The open
flow of his forms is held in check by the
geometry of the composition. Abstraction finally
is a composed, contained, and stabilized space
rather than a living and ever-changing kind of
activity. Kandinsky returns in his painting to a
primitive world which he wants to capture, while
Miró discovers a primitive world which is just
beginning, and which he is just beginning to
explore.

Harrison's essay is a good one, and it met the demands of
the particular assignment perfectly. (The students had been
asked to explore, through the analysis of two or three paintings,
some of the ways in which abstraction might convey meaning.)
You can also see, from the previous discussion of Pollock's
abstract compositions, that many of her arguments fit nicely into
a larger frame. She has identified, in fact, one of the major issues
of abstract art: is it a self-contained whole, "pure painting," or is
it a kind of ongoing process, an open form? It would not be very
difficult to convert Harrison's essay into a discussion of the possibilities of abstract painting in the twentieth century. To do so,
however briefly, would add to its richness.

Revising and Editing

Harrison needed to ask herself not only *what* these paintings mean in and of themselves—a question she has answered
very well—but *how* their meaning fits into the larger context of
art history. How do they reflect the age in which they were
created? She need not read widely in the theory of abstract art in
the twentieth century in order to fully develop her essay—
although, of course, it wouldn't hurt—but she needs only to
reflect a little on some of the things that she had undoubtedly
heard in class and read in her text about Miró and Kandinsky—
for instance, Miró's ties to the Surrealists, or some of Kandinsky's writings, such as the little book *Concerning the Spiritual in
Art*, which he had written in the first decade of the century in
Germany, or Kandinsky's experience with the Russian
Suprematists after the Revolution and his work at the Bauhaus
in Germany in the 1920s. These are all contexts which inform

the paintings and which would broaden the significance of Harrison's discussion.

I am suggesting that Harrison's essay could usefully undergo another *revision*. One of the great advantages of employing one of the preliminary writing exercises suggested is that it will get you in the habit of writing multiple drafts of a paper. As you move from the prewriting stage to a more formal version of your argument, you will see your ideas develop and change. You will write an even better paper, however, if you set aside your first draft of the final version and return to it later intent on revising your thinking once again. If you have the time, it is generally worth your while to revise your essay several times.

Revision demands that you be self-critical. It is different from editing, which is the last stage of the writing process. When you edit your final draft, you check for spelling mistakes, typos, proper punctuation, and so on. (Be sure, for instance, that the names of works of art are underlined.) Read the paper out loud. Doing this slows down the reading process, requires you to pay more attention than you otherwise might, and often reveals awkwardnesses that you can ignore when reading silently. Revision, on the other hand, is less mechanical and more conceptual. You need to recognize at what point your argument is weaker than it should be, where you fail to state your case as strongly as you might, when you've chosen a word that is too general or too vague. Also you need to take the time to make the correction. Most handbooks for writers have revision checklists that can help you think about the various elements of your essay. Here is a set of questions that are particularly appropriate for writing about art.

A Revision Checklist

The Essay as a Whole

1. Have you clearly stated and developed your thesis?
2. Have you focused on particular works of art in order to support your thesis?
3. Have you discussed these works of art in sufficient detail?
4. Have you adequately considered the significance or meaning of the works, as opposed to merely describing them?
5. Have you satisfactorily accounted for the title(s) of the work(s) of art you are discussing?

6. Have you considered how these works reflect larger art historical issues and tendencies?
7. Is your argument logical? Does it make sense?

Paragraphs

1. Does your introduction clearly state your thesis?
2. Are connections between paragraphs clear? Does one follow logically from the other?
3. Does your conclusion provide a satisfying sense of completion?
4. Are your paragraphs well developed? Does each contain concrete, specific examples in support of a general idea? Are these examples interesting and persuasive?
5. Have you quoted primary and secondary sources effectively?
6. Does quoted material further your *own* argument?
7. Have you avoided relying too heavily on outside sources?
8. Have you avoided concluding your paragraphs with quotations? (If not, this is a good indication that you are relying on others and not developing an argument of your own.)

Sentences and Words

1. Are facts, figures, and dates accurate?
2. Are footnotes accurate?
3. Have you footnoted all the material and ideas that you found in primary and secondary sources?
4. Are there consistently no more than two or three footnotes per typed page? (If there are more, this is another indication that you are relying too much on the thinking of others and not enough on your own ideas.)
5. Have you used exact words? Is your vocabulary describing formal elements, principles of design, and media and materials accurate?
6. Is your language concrete and specific rather than general and vague?
7. Is your choice of words properly formal? (You probably want to avoid slang and jargon.)
8. Have you avoided sexist language?
9. Have you avoided clichés?

A word of warning: you will be tempted to answer "yes" to all of these questions when you really mean "more or less." Don't let yourself get away with this. Not until you can answer "yes" in all honesty—when, that is, you are being honestly self-critical—will your paper finally be ready to hand in.

WRITING ABOUT ART:
THE FINAL PRODUCT

The following essay, by Sharon Lautenschlager, another student in a nineteenth-century painting survey course, expands upon its discussion of a particular painting—David's *Portrait of Madame Trudaine* (Fig.27)—just enough to make it resonate not only with David's other work of the period, but with the circumstances surrounding the French Revolution as a whole. In a very real sense the painting becomes as much a portrait of the Revolution itself as of a particular French woman. In fact, an interesting question was raised in the course of researching this paper in preparation for publication here: the painting is referred to in the scholarship sometimes as a portrait of *Madame Trudaine* but even more often as a portrait of one *Madame Chalgrin*. According to the Louvre, however, the painting is now believed to be a portrait of Madame Charles Louis Trudaine, born Micault de Courbeton, 1769–1802. The only way I can account for this discrepancy is to suggest that, in the confusion of the Revolution, even the identity of David's sitter was lost. Lautenschlager's essay seems to capture this spirit of contradiction and discrepancy. No great amount of learning was required for her to write it, and yet the paper seems convincing, even learned. It is an example of words and images coming together in a way that enriches them both. This is admittedly a very good paper. It has, furthermore, undergone several revisions, the last with considerable input from me in preparation for publication, so that I could provide you, in the end, with a "model" essay. But it remains, by and large, Lautenschlager's work, and it represents an example of writing about art that is not, I submit, beyond your reach.

Painting the Revolution:
David's <u>Portrait of Madame Trudaine</u>

Sharon Lautenschlager

The opening paragraph of Dickens' <u>Tale of Two Cities</u> ("It was the best of times; it was the worst of times") speaks eloquently of the essential contradictions and conflicts of the French Revolution. The <u>Portrait of Madame</u>

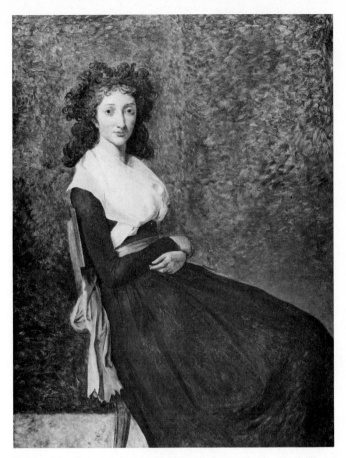

Figure 27　Jacques Louis David, *Madame Charles Louis Trudaine, born Micault de Courbetan* (1769–1802), sometimes known as *Madame Chalgrin*, 1791. Oil on canvas, 4 feet 3¼ inches by 3 feet, 2½ inches. Musée du Louvre, Paris. Courtesy the Réunion des musées nationaux.

<u>Trudaine</u>, painted by Jacques–Louis David in 1790–91, speaks as eloquently in visual terms of these same conflicts. This portrait is at the same time rigidly geometric and wildly passionate; it simultaneously pulls you in and pushes back at you; it is both coldly mathematical and warmly human. The composition is almost aggressively simple, and yet every element has been carefully contrived to create a specific kind of effect. Anita Brookner has said in her

study of David that "David did not influence the
Revolution; the Revolution influenced David."[1]
His Portrait of Madame Trudaine bears witness to
that influence.

Everything in this picture argues against
something else; but everything in the picture
also repeats and confirms something else. The
disturbing, unsettling impact is first created by
two devices, and close examination reveals
multitudes of other devices which serve to
maintain and enhance that original impact. One of
the major "contradictions" is the color. David
has painted this portrait with two sets of nearly
complementary colors--dark orange and green for
the larger color masses, and less intense blue
and yellow for the two smaller areas. These two
pairs of opposites, plus white, comprise the
total pallette of the picture. The second,
equally important contradiction is the contrast
between the absolute stillness of the sitter's
posture and expression, and the wild freedom of
the brushstroke throughout most of the picture, a
quality which cannot be dismissed as merely a
function of the painting's possibly "unfinished"
state since this same brushwork appears
throughout David's work in technically "finished"
paintings.[2]

The painting can be broken up into almost
endless geometric balances and repetitions,
parallels and perpendiculars, diagonals which
divide, angles which repeat one another, and
ovals and curves which appear over and over
again. For example, diagonals drawn from each
upper corner to each opposing lower corner would
intersect at the hands, which are thus precisely
centered top-to-bottom and side-to-side. The
right half of the painting consists of two
shapes, the background and the skirt of the
sitter's dress, both of which are painted without
dimension or detail, and which echo each other's
shape. Another pair of shapes, on the left side
of the painting, echo each other exactly in shape
and dimension, but oppose one another in color
and direction--these are the small yellow
rectangle of the floor, and the large orange

rectangle formed by a subtle but unmistakable value shift in the otherwise random "scumbling" of the background, which makes a vertical line running from the top of the canvas down to the sitter's hands. This barely perceptible line runs parallel to the sides of the frame, as does another implied line, formed by the sitter's nose, chin, the shadow line on the throat, the elbow, the sash, and finally the leg of the chair. The sash of the woman's dress has been strategically arranged to break up what would have been the curve at the back of the chair--a curve which could not have worked in the composition. A graceful or seductive tilt to the head would have been equally out of place here, so Madame Trudaine holds herself rigidly erect, with her face turned at an uncomfortably sharp angle to the body, with the eyes and mouth on a plane exactly parallel to the top and bottom of the frame, as well as the floor line. What cannot be made horizontal or vertical in the composition are curves in the face and hands, but these are made to repeat themselves. The oval of the face is the same oval as the left hand, and the same again as the eyes. The sharp curve of the end of the nose is the same curve as the end of the chin, and this angle is repeated in the crook of the arm and the end of the sash. The triangle between the chair leg and dress is repeated by shapes on the torso. This playing with line and shape could go on indefinitely.

Opposing this rigidly ordered geometry is the human element of the portrait. There is a very appealing frankness and openness in the expression of Madame Trudaine which is confirmed by the graceful curve of the visible hand and the enigmatic smile. While the unkempt hair and utter simplicity of the dress indicate a disarming absence of personal vanity, the sharply contrasted but modestly formed bodice indicates a gentle femininity that is very appealing. Balancing and opposing this warmth, however, is the rigidly upright and tightly self-contained pose which utterly denies any invitation to intimacy expressed in the face. Beyond the pose,

the composition conspires to push the figure out
aggressively at the viewer by the absence of any
perspectival depth. Not only has architectural
detail been eliminated (no corners, windows,
shadows of any kind), but even the cropping,
which eliminates any visible contact between the
chair and sitter with the floor, prohibits
orientation of Madame Trudaine in a logical
space. With nothing but a geometric grid to hold
her in place, the aggressive color of the
background pushes her forward. While the woman's
facial expression is warm and open, her body
language is rigid and self-contained. While the
composition is all order and simplicity, the
brushwork and color are all freedom and
extravagance. The effect is one of extreme
tension, or of passion restrained.

David produced this painting during the first
years of the Revolution, a year after Brutus and
the Lictors, and two years before Marat. At the
same time as this was painted, he was struggling
to finish The Tennis Court Oath. In his monograph
on David, Antoine Schnapper informs us that in
the Versailles sketchbook David has scrawled a
note to himself noting that the Trudaine brothers
had subscribed for two prints each of the
engraving of The Tennis Court Oath.[3] The younger
brother, Charles Michel, had commissioned The
Death of Socrates, and the elder, Charles Louis,
had just commissioned David's portrait of his
wife. The brothers were among David's most
devoted and interested patrons, and discussions
with the two and their circle of friends had
evidently been profoundly influential upon
David's conception of not only the Death of
Socrates but also the Oath of the Horatii.[4]
Nevertheless, as so often happened, on the eve of
the 9th Thermidor, in July 1794, the two brothers
were both guillotined.

The Portrait of Madame Trudaine is an intensely
emotional painting, deeply involved in the
passionate struggle to create a new order of
things and yet deeply conscious of the need to
submit these passions to order and discipline.
Her costume, as Norman Bryson has put it, "is

stridently republican. . . . Her strained impassive
expression and the resignation of her folded arms
indicate acceptance of the changing times; it is
almost the attitude of a person under arrest, a
person awaiting sentence."[5] Like <u>The Tennis Court
Oath</u>, the <u>Portrait of Madame Trudaine</u> is a
painting literally undone by history. If not
actually left unfinished by its subject's--and
society's--fall from grace, then it is painted so
as to feel unfinished, undone, the emblem of
change itself.

NOTES

1. Anita Brookner, <u>Jacques-Louis David</u> (New
York: Harper & Row, 1980), 82.

2. Jean Clay, in his <u>Romanticism</u> (New York:
Vendome Press, 1981), 121, notes the similarity
of this painting to David's <u>Portrait of Monsieur
de Joubert</u>, painted five years earlier, in 1786.
I have relied on the illustration in Clay's book
for my discussion of the painting's color.

3. Antoine Schnapper, <u>David</u>, trans. Helga
Harrison (New York: Alpine Fine Arts, 1980), 129.

4. Brookner, 83.

5. Norman Bryson, <u>Tradition and Desire: From
David to Delacroix</u> (Cambridge, England: Cambridge
University Press, 1984), 161.

NOTES

Introduction

1. Francine du Plessix Gray and Cleve Gray, "Who Was Jackson Pollock?" interviews with Lee Krasner, Anthony Smith, Betty Parsons, Alfonso Ossorio, *Art in America* 55 (May-June 1967): 51.

Chapter 1

1. Pierre Bourdieu and Alain Darbel, *L'Amour de l'Art* (Paris: Editions de Minuit, 1969), appendix 4, table 8.

2. Mina Loy, "Gertrude Stein," in *The Last Lunar Baedeker*, ed. Roger L. Conover (Highlands, NC: The Jargon Society, 1982), 298.

3. Brian O'Doherty, "Inside the White Cube: Notes on the Gallery Space," *Artforum* 14 (March 1976): 24–25.

4. Emile Zola, *The Masterpiece*, trans. Thomas Walton (Ann Arbor: University of Michigan Press, 1968), 128–29.

5. André Malraux, *Museum Without Walls*, trans. Stuart Gilbert and Francis Price (London: Secker & Warburg, 1967), 11–12.

Chapter 2

1. Joshua C. Taylor, *Learning to Look: A Handbook for the Visual Arts* (Chicago: University of Chicago Press, 1957), 44, 50.

2. Ibid., 52.

3. Quoted in Irving Stone, *Dear Theo: The Autobiography of Vincent Van Gogh* (New York: Doubleday, 1937), 383–84.

4. Quoted in Jacqueline and Maurice Guillaud, *Matisse: La rythme et la ligne* (Paris: Guillaud Editions, 1987), 24. All translations from this work are my own.

5. Stone, *Dear Theo*, 383.

6. Susan Sontag, *On Photography* (New York: Farrar Strauss & Giroux, 1977).

7. David Antin, "Video: The Distinctive Features of the Medium," in *Video Art* (Philadelphia: Institute for Contemporary Art, 1975), 64.

8. Guillaud, *Matisse*, 196.

9. Ibid., 75.

Chapter 3

1. "Unframed Space," in "The Talk of the Town," *New Yorker* 26 (August 5, 1950): 16.

2. Jackson Pollock, Statement, *Possibilities* 1 (1947), n.p.

3. Henry Adams, *The Education of Henry Adams*, ed. Ernest Samuels (Boston: Riverside Editions, 1973), 380, 382.

4. Robert Wohl, "The Generation of 1914 and Modernism," in *Modernism: Challenges and Perspectives*, ed. Monique Chefdor, Ricardo Quinones, and Albert Wachtel (Urbana: University of Illinois Press, 1986), 72.

5. These positions, and others as well, can be discovered in Francis Frascina, *Pollock and After: The Critical Debate* (New York: Harper & Row, 1985).

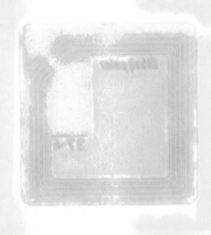